Contemporary Studies in Literature

Eugene Ehrlich, *Columbia University*
Daniel Murphy, *City University of New York*
  Series Editors

Virginia Woolf

a collection of criticism edited by Thomas S.W. Lewis

McGraw-Hill Book Company

New York • St. Louis • San Francisco • London • Paris • Düsseldorf
Tokyo • Kuala Lumpur • Mexico • Montreal • Pànama • São Paulo
Sydney • Toronto • Johannesburg • New Delhi • Singapore

123456789MUMU798765

Library of Congress Cataloging in Publication Data

Lewis, Thomas S W comp.
   Virginia Woolf: a collection of criticism

   (Contemporary studies in literature) (McGraw-Hill
paperbacks)
   Bibliography: p.
   1.   Woolf, Virginia Stephen, 1882–1941— Addresses,
essays, lectures.
PR6045.072Z78   823'.9'12   75-2048
ISBN 0-07-037540-2 pbk.

Preface

In the thirty-three years since Virginia Woolf drowned in a tidal river near her home in Sussex, England, the interest in her life, her writing, and her circle of friends, the "Bloomsbury Group," has increased steadily. Sales of her books (something she and her husband, Leonard Woolf, watched closely while they were alive) show that she is more popular today than ever before. As her popularity has increased so has the number of critical articles and books written about her work. Today Woolf afficionados may read two periodicals, *Virginia Woolf Quarterly* and *Virginia Woolf Miscellany*, and about thirty-five books devoted exclusively to her. Like Yeats, Joyce, and Faulkner, who have long had critical "industries," we may now speak of a Woolf "industry." How does one, reading Virginia Woolf for the first time, perhaps, begin the voyage out through the sea of critical articles and books? This collection of essays and the bibliography that follows should provide at least part of the answer.

In making the selections for this volume, I have endeavored to include the most intelligent recent criticism about Woolf's major works that will be of particular value to readers who are not Woolf specialists. With the exceptions of Louie Mayer's recollection of the author and Woolf's own essay, "Modern Fiction," the selections here deal with specific novels rather than with themes that run through her fiction. My only regret in choosing these essays is one I am sure I must share with other editors of similar collections: spatial limitations have made it necessary for me to exclude Morris Beja's "Virginia Woolf: Matches Struck in the Dark" (in *Epiphany in the Modern Novel*, Seattle, University of Washington Press, 1971). In addition, I feel that books like Harvena Richter's *Virginia Woolf: The Inward Voyage* (Princeton, Princeton University Press, 1970) and Mitchell Leaska's *Virginia Woolf's Lighthouse: A Study in Critical Method* (New York, Columbia

University Press, 1970) should be read in their entirety. To excerpt these volumes or to cut these articles would be a disservice to the authors.

Virginia Woolf's "Modern Fiction" is an essay that is a pleasure to read and reread. Published in 1919, a few months before her novel *Night and Day*, this essay contains a gentle attack on the limitations of the three most popular novelists of the day, H. G. Wells, John Galsworthy, and Arnold Bennett, accusing these writers of being "materialists"—concerned with the body rather than the spirit—and of making with "immense skill . . . the trivial and transitory appear true and enduring." (Bennett responded to this charge briefly by saying that Woolf did not create characters that survive, a comment that prompted her to write "Mr. Bennett and Mrs. Brown.") These novelists, Woolf contended, lacked the profundity of the great Russian writers, and they failed to experiment with form as Joyce had done. She then outlined what she felt to be the true job of the novelist, to look at life subjectively and to "record the atoms as they fall upon the mind." In my own essay on the short story "An Unwritten Novel," I examine one of Virginia Woolf's earliest attempts to put into practice the methods she speaks of in "Modern Fiction."

In compiling this volume, I have reread and hence rediscovered Winifred Holtby's *Virginia Woolf*, a book long out of print, which Carolyn Heilbrun described as "certainly the best book on Woolf written prior to 1960." I have chosen to reprint here Holtby's chapter on *Jacob's Room*, entitled "Cinematograph," in which she uses the metaphor of a movie scenario to explain one of Woolf's most difficult novels.

I am including essays about each of Mrs. Woolfs most popular works, *Mrs. Dalloway, To the Lighthouse,* and *Orlando.* Woolf's own introduction to the 1928 Modern Library edition of *Mrs. Dalloway,* which has been out of print for many years, makes interesting statements about the genesis of the novel. Lucio Ruotolo's essay presents an existentialistic interpretation of *Mrs. Dalloway.* Julia Carlson's hitherto unpublished essay on the solitary traveller passage demonstrates that it is integral to the rest of the novel. The selections dealing with *To the Lighthouse* concentrate on two of the central concerns of that work: Ruby Cohn discusses the place of art, and Carolyn Heilbrun considers the novel's androgynous elements. Joanne Trautmann's essay on *Orlando* together with the excerpts from Nigel Nicolson's *Portrait of a Marriage,* in which he reprints significant passages from the diary and letters of his mother, Vita Sackville-West, show the importance of biographical elements in Mrs. Woolf's mock biography.

The final three essays discuss Virginia Woolf's last novels. John Graham's article on *The Waves* presents an extensive discussion of

Woolf's use of tense and examines portions of an early draft. James Hafley's essay offers readers a provocative interpretation of *The Years*, a book that is not regarded by most critics as being one of her best. Hafley calls it "possibly the best and certainly one of the most interesting of Virginia Woolf's novels." Werner Deiman's essay, which deals substantially with *Between the Acts*, is one of the most perceptive pieces of general criticism about Virginia Woolf's last work.

I wish to thank Barbara Dacey, Ellin Sarot, Jan Young, and my wife, Jill, who have helped me both directly and indirectly in making the selections for this volume. Their suggestions have been valuable, and I am particularly grateful for their interest.

Thomas S. W. Lewis

Skidmore College
April 1975

Contents

Louie Mayer

Virginia Woolf: A Recollection

In the summer of 1934, when I was living at Southease in Sussex, I saw an advertisement in a local newspaper that particularly interested me: it said that a cook-general was wanted at a small country house near Lewes and that living accommodation—a cottage—would be provided rent-free. Replies were to be sent to Mrs. Woolf, Monks House, Rodmell. I was delighted to find this advertisement: it was the type of work I was looking for and my husband and I needed a cottage of our own. We also needed a school nearby for our children. I knew there was one at Rodmell, so I replied to the advertisement at once.

When I posted the letter I thought that perhaps nothing would come of it. As had happened before, I might not even have a reply. But within a few days, to my surprise, both Mr. and Mrs. Woolf came to see me. They must have read the letter when they came down to Rodmell for the weekend and then driven the few miles to Southease early the next morning.

They described to me the work I would do at Monks House in great detail. Mr. Woolf explained that their day was very carefully planned, almost hour by hour, and it was important nothing should happen that could alter their routine. I felt that they must be people who really loved time. Indeed I hoped that I would be able to keep to the hours they mentioned, but it did seem to be a rather alarming timetable. Mrs. Woolf then told me about the cottage. It was only "two up and two down" she said, but it was not far from the house and improvements would be made to it for whoever had the job.

A few days later Mrs. Woolf wrote to me—I can remember the letter well, it was written on bright green paper—she said that she would engage me and to begin with would pay me seven shillings and sixpence a week and that I could live in the cottage Mr. Woolf had bought in Rodmell. I was thrilled that the job was mine. In those days, seven shillings and sixpence a week and a cottage rent-free was really a big wage.

I was very young when I started work at Monks House and I wondered if I would be able to keep to so strict a timetable. I knew I could make a success of the job if I did the right thing at the right time. But I need not have worried: Mr. and Mrs. Woolf went to a lot of trouble to make me feel at home and help me adjust to their routine. I liked them both the very first week.

I had a long day's work, starting at eight in the morning and ending after nine at night, but in those days I—and my friends doing the same jobs—did not think of our day in terms of hours. We liked our work, we were proud to do it well, and I am afraid that we were very very happy. Although my husband also had an extremely busy day, he helped me by putting our two children to bed. I had some free time in the afternoon and was able to spend it with my family, but the children often came with me to Monks House. In fact I think they were practically brought up there in the kitchen; they ran in and out to the garden, helping Percy Bartholomew, Mr. Woolf's gardener, as if it was their own home.

There was one thing I found rather strange on my first day. The floors in Monks House were very thin, the bathroom was directly above the kitchen and when Mrs. Woolf was having her bath before breakfast I could hear her talking to herself. On and on she went, talk, talk, talk: asking questions and giving herself the answers. I thought there must be two or three people up there with her. When Mr. Woolf saw that I looked startled he told me that Mrs. Woolf always said the sentences out loud that she had written during the night. She needed to know if they sounded right and the bath was a good, resonant place for trying them out. He was so used to hearing her talk to herself in this way that he did not notice it at all. I became used to it too, but it startled me in the mornings for quite some time.

I was not allowed to make coffee at Monks House—Mr. and Mrs. Woolf were very particular about coffee and always made it themselves—so Mr. Woolf came into the kitchen at 8 o'clock every morning to make it. When we carried the breakfast trays to Mrs. Woolf's room I noticed that she had always been working during the night. There were pencils and paper beside her bed so that when she woke up she could work, and sometimes it seemed as though she had had very little sleep. These pieces of paper, some of them containing the same sentence written over and over again, would be in heaps about the room. They were on the chairs, on the tables and sometimes even on the floor. It was one of Mrs. Woolf's habits, when she was working, to leave her writing about in little heaps of paper. I would find them about the house too: in the sitting room and dining room on the tables and the mantelpieces.

Mrs. Woolf's bedroom was always outside the house in the garden; I used to think how inconvenient it must be to have to go out in the rain to go to bed. She also had a writing room in the garden, near her room, because it was quiet there and she could work undisturbed. Her bedroom had been added on to the back of the house; the door faced the orchard and a window at the side opened out on to a large field. I remember that a cow came one night and put its head in through the window. It amused Mrs. Woolf very much, but in case it happened again Mr. Woolf bought the field and added part of it to the garden. Then, because the writing room was small, he had a larger one built for her at the end of the garden against the church wall. When it was finished, Mrs. Woolf had a beautiful view eastwards across the meadows to Mount Caburn, and that is where she used to sit every day and work.

I can always remember her coming to the house each day from the writing room: when I rang the bell for lunch at 1 o'clock she used to walk down through the orchard smoking one of her favorite cigarettes in a long holder. She was tall and thin and very elegant. She had large, deep-set eyes and a wide curving mouth—I think perhaps it was this feature that made her face seem particularly beautiful. She wore long skirts—usually blue or brown corduroy—in the fashion of the day, and silk jackets of the same color. I remember, too, there was always a large silk handkerchief tucked into the jacket pocket.

Her cigarettes were made from a special tobacco called My Mixture. Mr. Woolf bought it for her in London and, in the evenings, they used to sit by the fire and make these cigarettes themselves. It was a mild sweet-smelling tobacco, and she would not have any other cigarettes, though sometimes she smoked a long thin cheroot which she enjoyed very much.

Mrs. Woolf wore clothes that suited her well, especially when she was going to a party. I pressed them for her and did any sewing that was necessary—she was not able to sew, although sometimes she liked to try. She liked trying to cook too, but I always felt that she did not want to give time to cooking and preferred to be in her room working.

But there was one thing in the kitchen that Mrs. Woolf was very good at doing: she could make beautiful bread. The first question she asked me when I went to Monks House was if I knew how to make it. I told her that I had made some for my family, but I was not expert at it. "I will come into the kitchen, Louie," she said, "and show you how to do it. We have always made our own bread." I was surprised how complicated the process was and how accurately Mrs. Woolf carried it out. She showed me how to make the dough with the right quantities of yeast and flour, and then how to knead it. She returned three or four times during the morning to knead it again. Finally, she made the dough into the shape of a cottage loaf and baked it at just the right temperature. I would say that Mrs. Woolf was not a practical person—for instance, she could not sew or knit or drive a car—but this was a job needing practical skill which she was able to do well every time. It took me many weeks to be as good as Mrs. Woolf at making bread, but I went to great lengths practicing and in the end, I think, I beat her at it.

I soon became interested in preparing all sorts of dishes at Monks House. Mr. and Mrs. Woolf did not like me to cook large meals, but they lived well and enjoyed good food. They particularly liked game—grouse and pheasant with well-made sauces. Puddings had to be very light and newly made, they were mostly *crèmes* and *soufflés*. I became so interested in cooking that Mrs. Woolf asked me if I would like to have lessons in advanced cooking at Brighton Technical College. I thought this was a wonderful idea, and so she arranged for me to have a year's course. I enjoyed the lessons enormously; every day I left Rodmell at eleven in the morning and returned late in the afternoon to cook dinner and experiment with the recipes I had been shown. By the end of the year I was able to prepare quite complicated dishes and to arrange a good menu when special guests came to Monks House—that is, when Mrs. Woolf was well enough for friends to come and see her.

Sometimes Mrs. Woolf was quite ill while working on a book and had acute headaches. Mr. Woolf then had to ration the number of friends who came to the house. Or, to those who did come, he had to say that she would only be able to talk to them for a short time. He did not like doing this but he knew that if she did not have enough rest she would become very ill. Of course, her relations who lived nearby came to see her all the time—particularly her sister Vanessa, and her niece Angelica. Mrs. Woolf was always delighted to see them. But, other than her relations, not many people who lived locally came to the house at any time. When Mrs. Woolf was well they invited special friends to stay, most of them lived in London.

Of their friends, I particularly remember Kingsley Martin. He came many times to Monks House and talked a great deal about politics with

Mr. Woolf. Mrs. Nicolson [Vita Sackville-West] used to come over from Sissinghurst and stay for the weekend. I liked her very much. She was tall and beautiful, and had a rather rosy face. Mrs. Woolf was always so pleased when she came to see her. I particularly remember Mr. Tom Eliot, too. He was a very gentle person, quiet and reserved, but he talked a lot of the time to Mrs. Woolf and sometimes she used to tease him and make him laugh. When he was staying for the weekend I always hurried over from my cottage on a Sunday morning to cook breakfast and then I would knock on Mr. Eliot's door to let him know it was ready, only to find that he had gone to church and his room was empty. Mr. and Mrs. Woolf never went to church, and it was difficult to remember that he went every Sunday.

Another frequent visitor was Dame Ethel Smyth. She was very amusing: she used to drive over to Rodmell in her funny old car, get out and then stand at the gate shouting for Mrs. Woolf. "Virginia!" she would yell at the top of her voice. She was deaf and did not know how much noise she was making. Dame Ethel not only came many times to Monks House, she also wrote a letter to Mrs. Woolf nearly every day. I used to collect the letters from the postman at my cottage in the morning—so that he would not wake Mr. and Mrs. Woolf too early—and Mrs. Woolf always asked me if there was one from Dame Ethel, I think she looked forward to her letters. When Mr. Woolf sat by her bed at breakfast time to drink coffee and talk to her, she used to read the letter to him and it amused them very much.

Mrs. Woolf was always delighted when she had finished writing a book, but the weeks following its completion were anxious ones for Mr. Woolf. He knew that she might have some sort of nervous reaction to the long hours of hard work and so become ill again. If she began to develop bad headaches and look really exhausted, he stopped all visitors coming to the house and insisted that she had complete rest. I knew when Mrs. Woolf's health was reaching this stage because she used to come into the kitchen and sit down and wonder what it was she had come to tell me. Then she would go out into the garden and walk about very slowly as though trying to remember. I have seen her bump into trees while she walked, not really knowing what she was doing. There were times, too, when she looked exhausted after they had driven down from London. I think this was usually in the winter when it was very cold. She hated to feel cold at any time: it seemed to affect her in a strange way—almost to frighten her. They used to sit by a log fire and drink coffee until she was warm and felt better.

I particularly remember Mrs. Woolf coming to my cottage one afternoon. I was surprised to see her hurrying down the road, because she seldom came to see me, and I thought she must have something special to say. When she had sat down, she said, "Louie, I have finished my book!" I knew then why she had come. She had been working for a long time on her novel *The Years,* and had been ill several times while trying to complete it. She was so delighted it was finished that she just had to come and tell someone. Then she said, "Now we are going to spend some money and have the kitchen painted and a lot of new things put in for you." She was so excited that we spent the rest of the afternoon making plans for the kitchen.

In spite of the exhaustion that Mrs. Woolf suffered while writing her books, I always felt that she must be quite strong physically. Even when she had been very ill—as she was during the last few months of writing *The Years*—she managed to recover after a long rest. She was impatient with being ill and, I think, showed great courage in her determination to be well as quickly as possible.

But early in 1941, after finishing her last novel, Mrs. Woolf was ill once more, and this time she seemed to have great difficulty in recovering. Mr. Wolf was so worried about her that he persuaded her to see a specialist in Brighton. This was something I had not known her do before. With the specialist's help and with the care Mr. Woolf took in seeing that she had as much rest as possible, she began to recover a little. One morning, when I was tidying Mr. Woolf's study, they both came into the room and Mr. Woolf said, "Louie, will you give Mrs. Woolf a duster so that she can help you clean the room?" He had been talking to her in her bedroom during the morning because it seemed to be one of her bad days again, and he must have suggested that she might like to do something, perhaps help with the housework. I gave her a duster, but it seemed very strange. I had never known her want to do any housework with me before. After a while Mrs. Woolf put the duster down and went away. I thought that probably she did not like cleaning the study and had decided to do something else.

Later in the morning I saw her come downstairs from the sitting room and go out to her room in the garden. In a few minutes she returned to the house, put on her coat, took her walking stick and went quickly up the garden to the top gate. She must have been writing a letter to Mr. Woolf and to her sister when she was in the sitting room, then left them on the little coffee table and rushed off like that so that we would not see her.

When I rang the bell at 1 o'clock to tell Mr. Woolf that lunch was ready, he said he was going upstairs to hear the news on the radio and would only be a few minutes. The next moment he came running down the stairs to the kitchen calling me, "Louie!" he said, "I think something has happened to Mrs. Woolf! I think she might have tried to kill herself! Which way did she go—did you see her leave the house?" "She went through the top gate a little while ago,'' I said. It was suddenly a terrible nightmare. We ran out into the garden and I went to find the gardener, in case he had seen Mrs. Woolf return. Mr. Woolf went to the top gate and ran down towards the river. The gardener had not seen Mrs. Woolf, so he went as fast as he could to find the policeman on duty in the village. They both went down to the river to see if they could help Mr. Woolf. He had found her walking stick stuck in the mud by the bank, but there was no sign of Mrs. Woolf. They looked for her for a long time but there was nothing to tell them where she was. Mr. Woolf wondered if she had left her stick there to mislead them and had perhaps gone up to Shepherd's Cottage. This was one of her favorite walks and it was possible she had gone that way so that she could be alone, not knowing really what she was doing. I went with him to Shepherd's Cottage, but she was not there. We went back and looked for her along the water meadows, and the river bank, and the brooks, until it was nighttime and we had to give up. There was nothing more that any of us could do.

Two weeks later a policeman came to the house to tell Mr. Woolf that her body had been found. Some children walking by the river from Lewes had seen her body washed into the side against the bank. He said that there were heavy stones in the pockets of her jacket and she must have put them there and then walked straight down into the river. And that was terrible. It was the most terrible thing I have known.

Virginia Woolf

Modern Fiction

In making any survey, even the freest and loosest, of modern fiction it is difficult not to take it for granted that the modern practice of the art is somehow an improvement upon the old. With their simple tools and primitive materials, it might be said, Fielding did well and Jane Austen even better, but compare their opportunities with ours! Their masterpieces certainly have a strange air of simplicity. And yet the analogy between literature and the process, to choose an example, of making motor cars scarcely holds good beyond the first glance. It is doubtful whether in the course of the centuries, though we have learnt much about making machines, we have learnt anything about making literature. We do not come to write better; all that we can be said to do is to keep moving, now a little in this direction, now in that, but with a circular tendency should the whole course of the track be viewed from a sufficiently lofty pinnacle. It need scarcely be said that we make no claim to stand, even momentarily, upon that vantage ground. On the flat, in the crowd, half blind with dust, we look back with envy to those happier warriors, whose battle is won and whose achievements wear so serene an air of accomplishment that we can scarcely refrain from whispering that the fight was not so fierce for them as for us. It is for the historian of literature to decide; for him to say if we are now beginning or ending or standing in the middle of a great period of prose fiction, for down in the plain little is visible. We only know that certain gratitudes and hostilities inspire us; that certain paths seem to lead to fertile land, others to the dust and the desert; and of this perhaps it may be worth while to attempt some account.

Our quarrel, then, is not with the classics, and if we speak of quarrelling with Mr. Wells, Mr. Bennett, and Mr. Galsworthy it is partly that by the mere fact of their existence in the flesh their work has a living, breathing, every-day imperfection which bids us take what liberties with it we choose. But it is also true that, while we thank them for a thousand gifts, we reserve our unconditional gratitude for Mr. Hardy, for Mr. Conrad, and in a much lesser degree for the Mr. Hudson, of *The Purple Land, Green Mansions,* and *Far Away and Long Ago.* Mr. Wells, Mr. Bennett, and Mr. Galsworthy have excited so many hopes and disappointed them so persistently that our gratitude largely takes the form of thanking them for having shown us what they might have done but have not done; what we certainly could not do, but as certainly, perhaps, do not wish to do. No single phrase will sum up the charge or grievance which we have to bring against a mass of work so large in its volume and embodying so many qualities, both admirable and the reverse. If we tried to formulate our meaning in one word we should say that these three writers are materialists. It is because they are concerned not with the spirit but with the body that they have disappointed us, and left us with the feeling that the sooner English fiction turns its back upon them, as politely as may be, and marches, if only into the desert, the better for its soul. Naturally, no single word reaches the centre of three separate targets. In the case of Mr. Wells it falls notably wide of the mark. And yet even with him it indicates to our thinking the fatal alloy in his genius, the great clod of clay that has got itself mixed up with the purity of his inspiration. But Mr. Bennett is perhaps the worst culprit of the three, inasmuch as he is by far the best workman. He can make a book so well constructed and solid in its craftsmanship that it is difficult for the most exacting of critics to see through what chink or crevice decay can creep in. There is not so much as a draught between the frames of the windows, or a crack in the boards. And yet—if life should refuse to live there? That is a risk which the creator of *The Old Wives' Tale,* George Cannon, Edwin Clayhanger, and hosts of other figures, may well claim to have surmounted. His characters live abundantly, even unexpectedly, but it remains to ask how do they live, and what do they live for? More and more they seem to us, deserting even the well-built villa in the Five Towns, to spend their time in some softly padded first-class railway carriage, pressing bells and buttons innumerable; and the destiny to which they travel so luxuriously becomes more and more unquestionably an eternity of bliss spent in the very best hotel in Brighton. It can scarcely be said of Mr. Wells that he is a materialist in the sense that he takes too much delight in the solidity of his fabric. His mind is too generous in its sympathies to allow him to spend much time in making things shipshape and substantial. He is a materialist from sheer goodness of heart, taking upon his shoulders the work that ought to have been discharged by Government officials, and in the plethora of his ideas and facts scarcely having leisure to realize, or forgetting to think important, the crudity and coarseness of his human beings. Yet what more damaging criticism can there be both of his earth and of his Heaven than that they are to be inhabited here and hereafter by his Joans and his Peters? Does not the inferiority of their natures tarnish whatever institutions and ideals may be provided for them by the generosity of their creator? Nor, profoundly though we respect the integrity and humanity of Mr. Galsworthy, shall we find what we seek in his pages.

If we fasten, then, one label on all these books, on which is one word, materialists, we mean by it that they write of unimportant things; that they spend immense skill and immense industry making the trivial and the transitory appear the true and the enduring.

We have to admit that we are exacting, and, further, that we find it difficult to justify our discontent by explaining what it is that we exact. We frame our question differently at different times. But it reappears most persistently as we drop the finished novel on the crest of a sigh—Is it worth while? What is the point of it all? Can it be that owing to one of those little deviations which the human spirit seems to make from time to time Mr. Bennett has come down with his magnificent apparatus for catching life just an inch or two on the wrong side? Life escapes; and perhaps without life nothing else is worth while. It is a confession of vagueness to have to make use of such a figure as this, but we scarcely better the matter by speaking, as critics are prone to do, of reality. Admitting the vagueness which afflicts all criticism of novels, let us hazard the opinion that for us at this moment the form of fiction most in vogue more often misses than secures the thing we seek. Whether we call it life or spirit, truth or reality, this, the essential thing, has moved off, or on, and refuses to be contained any longer in such ill-fitting vestments as we provide. Nevertheless, we go on perseveringly, conscientiously, constructing our two and thirty chapters after a design which more and more ceases to resemble the vision in our minds. So much of the enormous labour of proving the solidity, the likeness to life, of the story is not merely labour thrown away but labour misplaced to the extent of obscuring and blotting out the light of the conception. The writer seems constrained, not by his own free will but by some powerful and un-scrupulous tyrant who has him in thrall to provide a plot, to provide comedy, tragedy, love, interest, and an air of probability embalming the whole so impeccable that if all his figures were to come to life they would find themselves dressed down to the last button of their coats in the fashion of the hour. The tyrant is obeyed; the novel is done to a turn. But sometimes, more and more often as time goes by, we suspect a momentary doubt, a spasm of rebellion, as the pages fill themselves in the customary way. Is life like this? Must novels be like this?

Look within and life, it seems, is very far from being "like this." Examine for a moment an ordinary mind on an ordinary day. The mind receives a myriad impressions—trivial, fantastic, evanescent, or engraved with the sharpness of steel. From all sides they come, an incessant shower of innumerable atoms; and as they fall, as they shape themselves into the life of Monday or Tuesday, the accent falls differently from of old; the moment of importance came not here but there; so that if a writer were a free man and not a slave, if he could write what he chose, not what he must, if he could base his work upon his own feeling and not upon convention, there would be no plot, no comedy, no tragedy, no love interest or catastrophe in the accepted style, and perhaps not a single button sewn on as the Bond Street tailors would have it. Life is not a series of gig lamps symmetrically arranged; but a luminous halo, a semi-transparent envelope surrounding us from the beginning of consciousness to the end. Is it not the task of the novelist to convey this varying, this unknown and uncircumscribed spirit, whatever aberration or complexity it may display, with as little mixture of the alien and external as possible? We are not pleading merely for courage and sincerity; we are suggesting that the proper stuff of fiction is a little other than custom would have us believe it.

It is, at any rate, in some such fashion as this that we seek to define the quality which distinguishes the work of several young writers, among whom Mr. James Joyce is the most notable, from that of their predecessors. They attempt to come closer to life, and to preserve more sincerely and exactly what interests and moves them, even if to do so they must discard most of the conventions which are commonly observed by the novelist. Let us record the atoms as they fall upon the mind in the order in which they fall, let us trace the pattern, however disconnected and incoherent in appearance, which each sight or incident scores upon the consciousness. Let us not take it for granted that life exists more fully in what is commonly thought big than in what is commonly thought small. Any one who has read *The Portrait of the Artist as a Young Man* or, what promises to be a far more interesting work, *Ulysses,* * now appearing in the *Little Review,* will have hazarded some theory of this nature as to Mr.

*Written April 1919.

Joyce's intention. On our part, with such a fragment before us, it is hazarded rather than affirmed; but whatever the intention of the whole there can be no question but that it is of the utmost sincerity and that the result, difficult or unpleasant as we may judge it, is undeniably important. In contrast with those whom we have called materialists Mr. Joyce is spiritual; he is concerned at all costs to reveal the flickerings of that innermost flame which flashes its messages through the brain, and in order to preserve it he disregards with complete courage whatever seems to him adventitious, whether it be probability, or coherence or any other of these signposts which for generations have served to support the imagination of a reader when called upon to imagine what he can neither touch nor see. The scene in the cemetery, for instance, with its brilliancy, its sordidity, its incoherence, its sudden lightning flashes of significance, does undoubtedly come so close to the quick of the mind that, on a first reading at any rate, it is difficult not to acclaim a masterpiece. If we want life itself here, surely we have it. Indeed, we find ourselves, fumbling rather awkwardly if we try to say what else we wish, and for what reason a work of such originality yet fails to compare, for we must take high examples, with *Youth* or *The Mayor of Casterbridge*. It fails because of the comparative poverty of the writer's mind, we might say simply and have done with it. But it is possible to press a little further and wonder whether we may not refer our sense of being in a bright yet narrow room, confined and shut in, rather than enlarged and set free, to some limitation imposed by the method as well as by the mind. Is it the method that inhibits the creative power? Is it due to the method that we feel neither jovial nor magnanimous, but centred in a self which, in spite of its tremor of susceptibility, never embraces or creates what is outside itself and beyond? Does the emphasis laid, perhaps didactically, upon indecency, contribute to the effect of something angular and isolated? Or is it merely that in any effort of such originality it is much easier, for contemporaries especially, to feel what it lacks than to name what it gives? In any case it is a mistake to stand outside examining "methods." Any method is right, every method is right, that expresses what we wish to express, if we are writers; that brings us closer to the novelist's intention if we are readers. This method has the merit of bringing us closer to what we were prepared to call life itself; did not the reading of *Ulysses* suggest how much of life is excluded or ignored, and did it not come with a shock to open *Tristram Shandy* or even *Pendennis* and be by them convinced that there are not only other aspects of life, but more important ones into the bargain.

However this may be, the problem before the novelist at present, as we suppose it to have been in the past, is to contrive means of being free to set down what he chooses. He has to have the courage to say that what interests him is no longer "this" but "that": out of "that" alone must he construct his work. For the moderns "that," the point of interest, lies very likely in the dark places of psychology. At once, therefore, the accent falls a little differently; the emphasis is upon something hitherto ignored; at once a different outline of form becomes necessary, difficult for us to grasp, incomprehensible to our predecessors. No one but a modern, perhaps no one but a Russian, would have felt the interest of the situation which Tchekov has made into the short story which he calls "Gusev." Some Russian soldiers lie ill on board a ship which is taking them back to Russia. We are given a few scraps of their talk and some of their thoughts; then one of them dies and is carried away; the talk goes on among the others for a time, until Gusev himself dies, and looking "like a carrot or a radish" is thrown overboard. The emphasis is laid upon such unexpected places that at first it seems as if there were no emphasis at all; and then, as the eyes accustom themselves to twilight and discern the shapes of things in a room we see how complete the story is, how profound, and how truly in obedience to his vision Tchekov has chosen this, that, and the other, and placed them together to compose something new. But it is impossible to say "this is comic," or "that is tragic," nor are we certain, since short stories, we have been taught, should be brief and conclusive, whether this, which is vague and inconclusive, should be called a short story at all.

The most elementary remarks upon modern English fiction can hardly avoid some mention of the Russian influence, and if the Russians are mentioned one runs the risk of feeling that to write of any fiction save theirs is waste of time. If we want understanding of the soul and heart where else shall we find it of comparable profundity? If we are sick of our own materialism the least considerable of their novelists has by right of birth a natural reverence for the human spirit. "Learn to make yourself akin to people. . . . But let this sympathy be not with the mind—for it is easy with the mind—but with the heart, with love towards them." In every great Russian writer we seem to discern the features of a saint, if sympathy for the sufferings of others, love towards them, endeavor to reach some goal worthy of the most exacting demands of the spirit constitute saintliness. It is the saint in them which confounds us with a feeling of our own irreligious triviality, and turns so many of our famous novels to tinsel and trickery. The conclusions of the Russian mind, thus comprehensive and compassionate, are inevitably, perhaps, of the ut- most sadness. More accurately indeed we might speak of the inconclu- siveness of the Russian mind. It is the sense that there is no answer, that if honestly examined life presents question after question which must be left to sound on and on after the story is over in hopeless interrogation that fills us with a deep, and finally it may be with a resentful, despair. They are right perhaps; unquestionably they see further than we do and without our gross impediments of vision. But perhaps we see something that escapes them, or why should this voice of protest mix itself with our gloom? The voice of protest is the voice of another and an ancient civilisation which seems to have bred in us the instinct to enjoy and fight rather than to suffer and understand. English fiction from Sterne to Meredith bears witness to our natural delight in humour and comedy, in the beauty of earth, in the activities of the intellect, and in the splendour of the body. But any deductions that we may draw from the comparison of two fictions so immeasurably far apart are futile save indeed as they flood us with a view of the infinite possibilities of the art and remind us that there is no limit to the horizon, and that nothing—no "method," no experiment, even of the wildest—is forbidden, but only falsity and pretence. "The proper stuff of fiction" does not exist; everything is the proper stuff of fiction, every feeling, every thought; every quality of brain and spirit is drawn upon; no perception comes amiss. And if we can imagine the art of fiction come alive and standing in our midst, she would undoubtedly bid us break her and bully her, as well as honour and love her, for so her youth is renewed and her sovereignty assured.

Thomas S. W. Lewis

Vision in Time: Virginia Woolf's "An Unwritten Novel"

Of all Virginia Woolf's fiction, her short stories have received the least attention. Seldom discussed in detail by critics, these stories are usually dismissed in a line or two as "experiments" or "sketches"—Mrs. Woolf's early attempts to employ, on a limited scale, the themes and techniques of her more important novels.[1] The premise is, of course, true, but to view the stories only as experiments and to give them a cursory reading is to neglect their merits. One of these stories, "An Unwritten Novel," has never received the attentive reading that it deserves. In it Woolf discusses, in her indirect and subjective way, the problems she faces as a novelist, presents notes for an unwritten novel, and creates, in Minnie Marsh and James Moggridge, two characters who stand as models for characters in her later fiction. Written with that subtle sense of exhilaration and playfulness that is so much a part of her fiction, "An Unwritten Novel" stands as one of Virginia Woolf's best short stories.

Appearing first in the *London Mercury* in July 1920, "An Unwritten Novel" came after the artistic success of her first novel, *The Voyage Out* (1915), and the publication of her "most conventional" novel, *Night and Day* (1919). In spite of its flaws, particularly in its plot, *The Voyage Out* showed Mrs. Woolf's considerable abilities in the handling of character—especially in those terrifying chapters that deal with Rachel Vinrace's fever, delirium, and death. The process of writing the novel as

[1]See particularly Bernard Blackstone, *Virginia Woolf: A Commentary* (New York: Harcourt, Brace, 1949), p. 51.

15

well as fears for its critical reception brought Mrs. Woolf to insanity, to (as she described in *The Voyage Out*) "those interminable nights which do not end at twelve, but go on into double figures—thirteen, fourteen, and so on until they reach the twenties, and then the thirties, and then the forties. She realized that there is nothing to prevent nights from doing this if they choose."[2] Because of her mental problems, publication had to be delayed two years. After *The Voyage Out* Mrs. Woolf needed a change, so she turned to the "quiet and undisturbing"[3] (and altogether undistinguished) *Night and Day*. But this novel, with its linear plot and conventional characterization, was not enough; even before its completion she began experimenting with two short stories that are concerned with the problems of perception, "The Mark on the Wall" (the Hogarth Press's first publication in 1917) and "Kew Gardens" (1919). As the narrator in the first story perceives the mark on the wall, it changes from something concave (perhaps a nail hole) to something that projects from the wall (perhaps the head of a gigantic old nail), but the narrator's perceptions are destroyed at the end of the story when a male (who presents the world of fact) identifies the mark as a snail. Somewhat typically for Woolf, the man leaves to buy a newspaper after making his identification. As time changes (much in keeping with Henri Bergson's concept of *durée*), so does one's perception of the object. The second story, "Kew Gardens," presents a snail's eye view of the world about it. The intensity of the moment for the snail lies in the difficulties it encounters while climbing a leaf. At the same time, the snail is removed from the intensity of the moment that the human beings are experiencing above, so that from its perspective on the leaf, the snail is better able to view the mosaic of human relationships above.

In "An Unwritten Novel" Mrs. Woolf builds upon these concerns with human perception and humorously presents a labyrinth of hitherto uncharted machinations of the human mind. No longer is she subject to that "powerful and unscrupulous tyrant" (whom she wrote of in her essay "Modern Fiction") who constrains authors "to provide a plot, to provide comedy, tragedy, love, interest . . ."[4] to their fiction. Instead she feels free to record the "atoms as they fall upon the mind in the order in which they fall" and to "trace the pattern however disconnected and incoherent in appearance, which each sight or incident scores upon

---

[2]Quentin Bell cites this passage as well when discussing Woolf's mental illness. See *Virginia Woolf* (New York: Harcourt, Brace, 1972), vol. II, p. 11.

[3]Ibid., p. 42.

[4]Reprinted in *The Common Reader* (New York: Harcourt, Brace, 1953), p. 153. ("Modern Fiction" also appears in this volume.)

the consciousness."[5] The reader of "An Unwritten Novel" must work through the labyrinth of the novelist's mind, perceive with the novelist's eyes, and, to use a metaphor related to the story, must reconstruct and make whole the pieces of the fragile eggshell, with little assistance from the conventional concepts of plot, characterization, and linear development.

"An Unwritten Novel"[6] is set in a railway carriage of a train traveling between London and Eastbourne. Opposite the narrator (Mrs. Woolf in my reading of the story) are five passengers, four of whom are doing those things people so often do to shield themselves from life —reading the *Times,* studying a map of the rail line, smoking, checking entries in a pocket book. It is the fifth person, an "unhappy woman," who, the narrator conjectures, looks at life directly. As the train stops at the various stations along the route, the other passengers depart until there are but three left—the narrator, the woman opposite, and a man reading the *Times.* When the train arrives at Three Bridges Station, the narrator speculates: "Was he going to leave us? I prayed both ways—I prayed last that he might stay. At that instant he roused himself, crumpled his paper contemptuously, like a thing done with, burst open the door, and left us alone." The one barrier between the narrator and the woman, a male who lives in the factual world of the *Times* (which he must crumple), leaves. The two are free now to enjoy (at least in the narrator's mind) their communion.

The narrator has not been without her own shield from life, a copy of the *Times* folded in a perfect square, but this proves to be of little value against the woman's gaze. Combined with that gaze the woman has a nervous twitch that makes her pluck the middle of her back, and as she speaks she fidgets as though "the skin on her back were as a plucked fowl's in a poulterer's shop window." When the woman tries to rub a spot off the window, the narrator follows suit, and then the spasm goes through the narrator: she too has the skin of a damp chicken. At this point, a "smile of infinite irony, infinite sorrow, flitted and faded from her face. . . . she had communicated, shared her secret, passed her poison; she would speak no more." In the narrator's mind a communion has taken place, and now the narrator is free to become a novelist and allow her own mind to create a life for the woman opposite. The rest of the story alternates between the subjective vision of the novelist and the objective reality of the woman opposite; it is specifically the tension between vision

[5]Ibid., p. 155.
[6]The story is reprinted in *A Haunted House and Other Stories* (New York: Harcourt, Brace, 1949), pp. 8–21.

and reality which allows Mrs. Woolf to explore questions of time, space, point of view, and character—questions that are so important to her particular conception of the universe.

In the first vision of her novelist, Mrs. Woolf makes the woman into Minnie Marsh, who is visiting her sister-in-law, Hilda, at Eastbourne. While there, she prays to a god molded not in the benevolent image of a Prince Albert but rather in the stern, authoritarian image of a Paul Kruger (who was not without his own delusions of divinity when he was president of the Transvaal in the nineteenth century). Minnie's prayers are for the expiation of a sin—and at this point the novelist assigns her the banal sin of having allowed her younger brother to scald himself to death while she lingered at a draper's shop. The god Kruger relentlessly drives her to the edge of sanity. When Minnie leaves Hilda's house for a walk along the pier at Eastbourne, the novelist is about to move the hapless woman "over the waterfall, straight for madness." But at this point the woman opposite brings the novelist back to reality and dispels the subjective vision by saying "eggs are cheaper." Minnie Marsh is not a person near bedlam, not someone driven by sublimated past crimes, but an utterly pedestrian person. The novelist can only return her to Hilda's house: "So she reaches home—scrapes her boots."

Since novelists must be concerned with craft as well as vision, Mrs. Woolf must face the central problem of the novelist's role in the story: "Have I read you right?"—a question that simply cannot be answered by a view of the woman's face which "holds more, withholds more." The answer lies, instead, in metaphor. Just as the artist thinks she has captured the moment (grasping the stem of the flower), time shifts the subject and the woman projects another side of herself ("the butterfly's off"). Charles Steele, the painter in *Jacob's Room,* encounters the same difficulty when Mrs. Flanders moves from the scene that he is painting: "Here was that woman moving—actually going to get up—confound her!" And it is related to the larger problem of those demons who get in between Lily Briscoe's vision and her canvas at the beginning of *To the Lighthouse.* Like the boat that Jacob Flanders sees moving across the horizon as he looks from the Durrants' dining room window, so time must change the moment in the railway car. The most the novelist can hope for as she surveys the scene is to be the hawk, to hover over the down, and to hold in stasis the "life, soul, spirit, whatever you are of Minnie Marsh." Yet time does change, the hawk is downed, when Minnie Marsh takes a hard-boiled egg from her bag and proceeds to peel off its shell. The same eggshell becomes one of the best metaphors for understanding her problem: "fragments of a map—a puzzle. I wish I could piece them together! If you would only sit still. She's moved her knees—the map's in bits again." It is the shell that serves as a vehicle for returning the novelist to her vision. Subjective visual perception takes hold once again as the fragments become boulders of marble falling in the Andes, crushing a troop of Spanish muleteers with their convoy of Drake's booty.

In the second vision, Mrs. Woolf's novelist has Minnie Marsh meet an "unborn child of the imagination," James Moggridge, a commercial traveler who takes his meals at Hilda's house each Thursday. Partly concealed from Minnie by the fronds of aspidistra that form the center-piece at the dinner table, Moggridge is free to watch her twitch and to ruminate on her spinsterhood. In the meantime Mrs. Woolf is free to view the Moggridge household: "his passion? Roses—and his wife a retired hospital nurse. . . ." Moggridge, "life's fault," must be in every novel; and the novelist submits to life's tyranny willingly: "I come irresistibly to lodge myself somewhere on the firm flesh, in the robust spine, wherever I can penetrate or find foothold on the person, in the soul, of Moggridge the man." But the Moggridges of the world, usually males in Virginia Woolf's world, stick to schedules and facts—and this particular Moggridge must leave the novel to meet his train.

At this point comes that delicate transition (so necessary for a novelist like Mrs. Woolf) from James Moggridge to Minnie Marsh, a transition that must be made at the expense of the moment. "One moment," the novelist thinks, "I'll linger," reminding us of the time Mrs. Ramsay savors as she looks over her shoulder into the dining room where she had created the moment of beauty at the dinner table; but of course for the creator of the dinner party and the creator of James Moggridge, the moment is "already the past."[7] The "atoms reassemble," a phrase that she borrows from "Modern Fiction"—and she returns Minnie Marsh to her room at the top of the house, to confront the "shrunken shreds of all the vanishing universe—love, life, faith, husband, children. . ." as she darns a grey wool glove. Like Mrs. Dalloway, who at fifty-two confronts a vanishing universe when she mends her dress, Minnie Marsh, too, faces a crisis. She must confront her sister-in-law, Hilda, and the Niagara of madness that lies ahead. But here the vision ends for the novelist because linear time interferes with her mind's projection; the train arrives at Eastbourne. The reality of the arrival is not without its irony, for it turns Minnie Marsh from the spinster of the novelist's mind into a mother being met by her son. "What do I stand on?" the novelist asks. "What do I know? That's not Minnie. There

---

[7]Quoted from *To the Lighthouse* (New York: Harcourt, Brace, 1955), p. 168. Earlier at the dinner table (p. 157) Mrs. Ramsay is described as hovering "like a hawk suspended."

never was a Moggridge. Who am I? Life's bare as a bone." The crisis is
the artist's, not the woman's. Mrs. Woolf and her novelist face it the only
way an artist can, by continuing to create. New questions form about
mother and child ("Who are you?"); undoubtedly these will lead to new
visions. It is the artist who moves to the sea at Eastbourne, where, before
the grey landscape and the murmuring fluidity of the waves, she reaffirms
her steadfast desire to create: "If I fall on my knees, if I go through the
ritual, the ancient antics, it's you unknown figures, you I adore; if I open
my arms, it's you I embrace, you I draw to me—adorable world!"

While such a short and necessarily reductive analysis of this complex story may well be dismissed as the sort of factual summation that
Mrs. Woolf would deplore, such a review does help to focus on several of
those concerns that are central both to this story and to Woolf's later
fiction, namely, the understanding of character and the function of time
both in her fiction and in her life. In this story she combines the two
concerns in an attempt to delineate the limitations imposed by time and
perspective on the comprehension of character.

There are at least two kinds of time present in Virginia Woolf's
fiction: linear, chronological time that eternally and inexorably moves
forward and what I choose to call "spherical time"—that fluid fourth
dimension in which the novelist has her visions and imposes order on the
chaos of linear time. Linear time encompasses all of life—so the sun rises
and sets in *The Waves,* and so Rhoda in that novel fears falling from the
"loop of time" into spherical visions. In "An Unwritten Novel," the
action takes place in a railway carriage, which, Mrs. Woolf is careful to
let us know, moves in a linear fashion across the landscape from London
to Eastbourne making its appointed stops along the way. Spherical time is
the novelist's visionary world, the world in which she makes order of her
life. Spherical time merges pasts and futures with the present and allows
the novelist to create her children of the mind.

Such remarks about Mrs. Woolf's handling of time in her fiction
have been made by others (though with different terms), but a few
remarks are in order concerning Mrs. Woolf's use of time in "An
Unwritten Novel" because the interaction of the two worlds of time
directly affects the way in which she sees her characters, at a specific,
created time of the novelist, at three o'clock on a December afternoon.

The novelist views the woman opposite and essentially embellishes
what she sees—the face that holds and withholds so much and the
dreadful twitch; from these two physical characteristics she creates a
character and so makes order for her mind. The novelist's creation takes
place in spherical time, but in a visionary world that never can be
divorced from the tyranny of linear time. It is the woman who twitches,

who interrupts the vision by removing the shell from a hard-boiled egg, and who leaves the train at Eastbourne, and it is the distinctions between linear and spherical time that so interest Mrs. Woolf. "[Yes, Minnie; I know you've twitched, but one moment—James Moggridge.]" says the novelist seeking to extend the hiatus of spherical time. Like the hawk, she wishes to continue floating on the thermal over the down. Yet the hawk, as she makes clear, is downed; linear time always intrudes.

Just as there are limitations imposed on the novelist by linear time, so there are limitations imposed by perspective. The hawk has a different view of the world from that of the snail and from that of people who walk in Kew Gardens. But, of course, to borrow Mrs. Woolf's words in her introduction to *Mrs. Dalloway*, "the truth that lies behind those immense facades of fiction" must be different if "life is indeed true and fiction is indeed fictitious."[8] By changing one's perspective, one comes closer to the truth.

Though a child of the mind and thus a child of Mrs. Woolf's spherical vision, James Moggridge lives in a world of timetables and chronos. A traveler in buttons, Moggridge bears some resemblance to Gerald Scales of Arnold Bennett's *The Old Wives' Tale*, but Mrs. Woolf is not content to give only an external view of Moggridge, as Bennett might have done. Wishing to discover the soul of this man who has organized himself so well in the world of linear time, she projects herself into his stomach: "while from above meat falls in brown cubes and beer gushes to be churned to blood again." Again, linear time intrudes, Minnie twitches, and James must leave the story and meet a train.

Most critics of Woolf tend to read her work with a high seriousness and neglect to mention the tremendous sense of playfulness that pervades so much of her writing. "An Unwritten Novel" is no exception. In *The Glass Roof*, James Hafley perceptively remarks that the story is "significant in its burlesque of Freud."[9] Citing the woman's twitch and the novelist's speculation about the God sending it to Minnie for a past crime, Hafley describes "An Unwritten Novel" as the most "amusing" of all Mrs. Woolf's stories. The burlesque goes even further than Freud, for Mrs. Woolf parodies those people who inhabit the novels that Arnold Bennett was so famous for, and she plays with themes that Bennett used so skillfully. As mentioned above, James Moggridge is loosely related to Gerald Scales. That Minnie allows her brother to die while lingering at a draper's shop seems more than coincidental with Sophia of *The Old*

---

[8]Mrs. Woolf's introduction to *Mrs. Dalloway* (reprinted in this volume) appeared in the Modern Library edition of 1928, p. vi.

[9]*The Glass Roof: Virginia Woolf As Novelist* (Berkeley: University of California Press, 1954), p. 47.

Wives' Tale, who allows her father to die when she lingers in the draper's shop. There is in these passages a humorous approach to the characters which is missing in Bennett. Other passages in the story suggest the gaiety of *Flush* and *Orlando*: eggshells become rockslides, a wooden cow (with intimations of Passaphae and the minotaur—associations that would not be lost on Mrs. Woolf) saves the woman from an indiscretion, and even at the end, when life is as bare as a bone, we are left with the joke that the woman is a mother and not a spinster.

Like "Kew Gardens," "The Mark on the Wall," "Monday or Tuesday," and "The String Quartet," there is a fluidity to "An Unwritten Novel" which is so much a part of Mrs. Woolf's later fiction. Early in 1920, Virginia Woolf wrote in her diary of a "new form for a new novel":

> Suppose one thing should open out of another—as in an unwritten novel—only not for 10 pages but for 200 or so—doesn't that give the looseness and lightness I want; doesn't that get closer and yet keep form and speed, and enclose everything, everything? My doubt is how far it will enclose the human heart—Am I sufficiently mistress of my dialogue to net it there? For I figure that the approach will be entirely different this time: no scaffolding; scarcely a brick to be seen; all crepuscular, but the heart, the passion, humor, everything as bright as fire in the mist. Then I'll find room for so much—a gaiety—an inconsequence—a light spirited stepping at my sweet will. Whether I'm sufficiently mistress of things—that's the doubt; but conceive (?) *Mark on the Wall, K. G.* and *Unwritten Novel* taking hands and dancing in unity. What the unity shall be I have yet to discover; the theme is a blank to me; but I see immense possibilities in the form I hit upon more or less by chance two weeks ago.[10]

All of Mrs. Woolf's great characters—Jacob Flanders, Lily Briscoe, and Mrs. Dalloway, to name but three—inhabit the crepuscular world Mrs. Woolf speaks of so elegantly here. In the reader's mind, they do shine as brightly as fire in the mist. Minnie Marsh and the narrator in "An Unwritten Novel" serve as forerunners of these great characters and help to make the story one of Virginia Woolf's best.

---

[10]Quoted from *A Writer's Diary* (New York: Harcourt, Brace, 1954), p. 22.

Winifred Holtby

Cinematograph: On Jacob's Room

In 1922, the year following *Monday or Tuesday*, Mrs. Woolf published *Jacob's Room*. It is her war book. It is as much a war book as *The Death of a Hero* or *Farewell to Arms*; yet it never mentions trenches, camps, recruiting officers, nor latrines. It does not describe the hero's feelings on the eve of battle; not an inch of barbed wire decorates its foreground. These things, of course, are relevant to modern war, but Mrs. Woolf does not describe them. She knew, perhaps, that her talent is unsuited to the description of violence in action, though she can measure with extraordinary range and accuracy its effect when action has ceased.

She lacks the particular type of imagination which enables Naomi Mitchison, for instance, to enter so freely the consciousness of her combative barbarians. She could not know in what terms Tommies referred to their sergeant-major nor what it feels like to thrust a bayonet through a belly. What she did know, what she could imagine, was what life looked like to those young men who in 1914 and 1915 crossed the Channel and vanished out of English life for ever. When such a young man was killed, she seems to ask, what was lost then? What lost by him? What was lost by his friends? What exactly was it that had disappeared?

In *Jacob's Room* she answers, "It was this."

The theme of the novel is the same as that of *The Voyage Out*. It is the masculine counterpart of that feminine story. Rachel Vinrace was educated for a life which led to premature death in South America; Jacob Flanders was educated for life which led to premature death in battle. The

"Cinematograph: On Jacob's Room" *by Winifred Holtby from* Virginia Woolf *(Wishart & Co., 1952, and Cedric Chivers, 1974), reprinted by permission of the author's literary executor, Paul Berry.*

theme of the two books is identical; but their treatment is altogether different. In *Jacob's Room* Mrs. Woolf built for the first time a complete novel with her new tools, and chose for it the cinematograph technique tried out in *Kew Gardens*. Almost any page in the book could be transferred straight on to a film. The story deals mainly with the external evidence of emotions, even thoughts and memories assuming pictorial quality. Sometimes, it is true, the action passes to that confused twilight which dwells within the mind; but for the most part it is indicated by the changing positions and gestures of the characters. Betty Flanders weeps, strokes the cat Topaz, writes letters; Jacob yawns, stretches, reads; Florinda draws her cloak about her to hide the evidence of her pregnancy. It is a picture-maker's novel.

It is not a perfectly easy book to read. Its obscurity puzzled a good many intelligent people when it was published, for Mrs. Woolf gives no clue to her intention. There is no preliminary announcement, as on a film, "Produced by ———. Scenario by ———. From the story of ———." But the first chapter betrays her method. Its scenario might be summarized, "Jacob as a small boy at the seaside in Cornwall," and Mrs. Woolf begins, as any producer might, by photographing a letter, word by word welling out slowly from the gold nib of Betty Flanders' pen. "So of course there was nothing for it but to leave." She shows us next the complete figure of the woman pressing her heels deeper in the sand to give her matronly body a firmer seat; then there is a close-up of her face, maternal, tearful, because Scarborough, where Captain Barfoot is, seems so far from Cornwall where she sits writing. The camera swings round then to photograph the entire bay, yacht and lighthouse, quivering through her tears, and flashes back to indicate a blot spreading across the writing paper.

There are two little boys, Archer and Jacob; but Archer cannot find Jacob, who has a habit of wandering off by himself, and Betty Flanders' mind—and the film—return to the situation which caused the tears to flow, Seabrook Flanders' death. Betty Flanders has been a widow for two years. She lives in Scarborough with her sons, and the rector's wife thinks in church, looking at her when the organ plays, that "marriage is a fortress and widows stray solitary in the open fields, picking up stones, gleaning a few golden straws, lonely, unprotected, poor creatures."

Ferreting in her bag for a stamp, rising to go, Betty Flanders disturbs the painter, Charles Steele, who was using her figure to balance the colors of his landscape. Archer runs across, shouting "Ja-cob! Ja-cob!" and Mrs. Flanders picks up her parasol.

But Jacob is off by himself, climbing a rock, teasing a crab, running away from a couple of trippers stretched on the sand, and comforting himself for the desolation of being alone, by the sight of a skull, "perhaps a cow's skull, a skull perhaps, with the teeth in it," lying under the cliff.

The picture moves on, showing Betty Flanders leading her children back to their lodgings, forgetting the meat, and greeting the maid, Rebecca. It shows the bare sitting room of the lodgings by lamplight, the light streaming through the window into the wet garden, lighting up a child's bucket and a purple aster drenched in the rain. It shows the children in bed, Archer wakeful, Jacob asleep with the sheep's jawbone at his feet. Mrs. Flanders soothes Archer frightened by the storm by telling him that the steamer won't sink. " 'The Captain's in bed long ago. Shut your eyes, and think of the fairies, fast asleep, under the flowers.' " The details of that composition are to be used again in *To the Lighthouse*—the bare, sea-surrounded bedroom, the children in bed, the skull, and Mrs. Ramsay soothing the wakeful Cam, telling her how lovely the skull looks now with her shawl draped round it; "how the fairies would love it; it was like a bird's nest; it was like a beautiful mountain such as she had seen abroad, with valleys and flowers and bells ringing and birds singing and little goats and antelopes. . . ." There is a dreamlike quality about it, as of a memory from early childhood, impressed upon the mind of a sensitive, nervous child by an understanding mother. It tranquilizes the picture, befitting the external vision of Mrs. Flanders and Rebecca bending over the cot of the smallest child, "conspirators plotting the eternal conspiracy of hush and clean bottles."

The section closes with a return to the rain-washed garden, and the crab caught by Jacob, vainly trying to escape from its bucket-prison, "trying again and falling back, and trying again and again."

The combination of elements here is masterly—Betty Flanders' care for her children, and her helplessness; Jacob's running off alone so that Archer must call after him, " 'Ja-cob! Ja-cob!' " his voice having "an extraordinary sadness. Pure from all body, pure from all passion, going out unto the world, solitary, unanswered, breaking against rocks—so it sounded." So, all through the book, Betty Flanders is to care for her children—and be impotent; so Jacob is to go off adventuring alone, till he adventures out of life altogether at the end; so, in his empty rooms, in the last chapter, his friend Bonamy is to call, " 'Jacob! Jacob!' " and no Jacob will answer. Only Mrs. Flanders, bursting open the bedroom door, holds up a pair of Jacob's shoes and asks. " 'What am I to do with these, Mr. Bonamy?' " and to that question there is, indeed, no satisfactory answer. The picture seems to compose a sort of refrain to the novel. It leaves an impression of apprehension, of the solicitude of women and of the indifference of fate which abandons opal-shelled crabs to the mercilessness of children, and abandons children to the mercilessness of war. Its melancholy, its extraordinary desolation, are indefinable.

The next chapter shows both Mrs. Woolf and her method at their worst. The scene is laid in Scarborough. The people are Betty Flanders and her neighbors; Captain Barfoot, an almost purely "literary" figure; a vague Rector's wife; a lovesick curate. Jacob himself, a schoolboy, collecting butterflies, is less definite here than elsewhere. Mrs. Woolf is clearly not at home in this provincial bourgeois household. Nobody comes to life.

One stroke in her portrait of Betty Flanders, however, is noteworthy, and that is the incident of Mr. Floyd, the curate, who proposed to her, and whom she did not like, because he had red hair. When he leaves for a parish in Sheffield, being unable to endure Scarborough, one imagines, after his rejection, he gives John Flanders a kitten; and years afterwards, when Betty reads in the *Scarborough and Harrogate Courier* that the Rev. Andrew Floyd has been made Principal of Maresfield House, she gets up and goes over to the fender and strokes the cat, whose fur was the color of Mr. Floyd's hair.

" 'Poor old Topaz,' said Mrs. Flanders, as he stretched himself out in the sun, and she smiled, thinking how she had had him gelded, and how she did not like red hair in men. Smiling, she went into the kitchen."

Now that, with its delicately suggested hint of cruelty and coarseness in a good and simple woman, has shocked many of Mrs. Woolf's admirers. But it is true. Good women frequently would be shocked to recognize their own motives. Betty Flanders quite probably would have derived satisfaction from her vicarious gelding of Mr. Floyd. As the episode stands, it gives a queer flavor of pungency to a picture which might otherwise have been too smooth and sweet.

There is one other interesting passage in the chapter, revealing that interrelationship of all Mrs. Woolf's novels which gives the impressive sense of unity to her work. Seabrook Flanders is dead. His widow has put on his tombstone "Merchant of this City" to impress the boys rather than to record a truth, for Seabrook had been in life a rolling stone, and only sat for three months behind an office window. But Betty, looking at the grave, wonders what he had been. "Had he then been nothing? An unanswerable question, since even if it weren't the habit of the undertaker to close the eyes, the light so soon goes out of them. At first, part of herself, now one of a company, he had merged in the grass, the sloping hillside, the thousand white stones, some slanting, others upright, the decayed wreaths, the crosses of green tin, the narrow yellow paths

. . . Seabrook was now all that; and when, with her skirt hitched up, feeding the chickens, she heard the bell for service or funeral, that was Seabrook's voice—the voice of the dead.'' What is it? What is it? Her mind reiterates. What happens to the dead? For what is life? Is Seabrook now like Wordsworth's Lucy—

> "No motion has she now, no force;
>   She neither hears nor sees;
> Rolled round in earth's diurnal course
>   With rocks and stones and trees"?

Is he like Virginia Woolf's Mrs. Ramsay in *To the Lighthouse?* Who, after she was dead, still left her shawl hanging from the skull in the children's bedroom, protective even in death, till it loosened itself, corner by corner, "with a roar, with a rupture, as after centuries of quiescence a rock rends itself from the mountain and hurtles crashing into the valley.'' Mrs. Ramsay is dead, rolled round with rocks and stones and trees. Her shawl, so soft, so protective, yet becomes part of that unity, that impersonal universe. Like a rock it falls. It crashes into the valley. In and in works the unifying mind, seeking, as Keats sought in his metaphors, as Shakespeare sought, as Wordsworth sought, some binding unity, some permanent and satisfying relationship between life and death and rocks and people.

If the Scarborough chapter is, apart from its relationship to Mrs. Woolf's ideas of life and death, a little dull and obscure, the Cambridge chapter is pure magic. Cambridge glows with all the romantic glamour with which her imagination might have invested it had she seen it first when she was young and impressionable, and had spent a wonderful May Week with her brothers. The method employed is still the method of the cinema.

Picture follows picture, each one touched with an almost unearthly glamour. The train to Cambridge, a service at King's College, the comic lunch with a don, the river, the quadrangle—they are entrancing. It is true that though Mrs. Woolf might be in love with Cambridge, she was not overmuch impressed by its high-priests. "It is not simple or pure, or wholly splendid, the lamp of learning,'' she informs us. The old men, whose heads are so full of knowledge, are, as often as not, twisted and queer as cactuses. Huxtable cannot walk straight after his port. Sopwith praises the sky, night after night, for twenty years. Cowan chuckles at the same stories. Learning can sometimes be, Mrs. Woolf insists, at odds with art. Learning can sometimes degenerate into superstition. Learning by no means always makes for wisdom. One is reminded of that passage in *The Mark on the Wall* when she reflects how admirable the world might be without specialists or learned men. She is affected too, partly perhaps, by the prohibitions which she describes in *A Room of One's Own*—prohibitions which order women out of libraries and off the grass. Yet her pictures of the dons themselves—Sopwith, Huxtable and Cowan—are admirably done, with justice and understanding as well as humor—especially the picture of Sopwith, to whom a man could say anything, who sat in his room, cutting cake, talking to undergraduates.

Mrs. Woolf can be just even where she has no particular liking; but where she likes, her pictures become radiant. The May air of the Cambridge spring, when Jacob escapes from the luncheon party and sculls up the river with Tim Durrant; Neville's Court by night, the windowboxes foaming with flowers, the window lit; Jacob's room, with its round table, low chairs, yellow flags in a jar on the mantlepiece, his essay manuscript, his notes, his pipes—these are pure poetry. The young men meet and argue about Keats. Jacob comes to the window. ''He looked satisfied; indeed masterly, which expression changed slightly as he stood there; the sound of the clock conveying to him (it may be) a sense of old buildings and time; and himself the inheritor; and then to-morrow; and friends; at the thought of whom, in sheer confidence and pleasure, it seemed, he yawned and stretched himself.'' We are reminded, by this tragic confidence, of Rachel and Terence, who were equally assured of life, equally doomed.

> ''Well, Rachel,'' Terence said, after drawing a picture of their future life together in London, ''we shall be doing that together in six weeks' time, and it'll be the middle of June then,—and June in London—my God! How pleasant it all is!''
>
> ''And we're certain to have it too,'' she said. ''It isn't as if we were expecting a great deal—only to walk about and look at things.''

''Certain to have it?'' With death always imminent? Jacob was certain. The others left him alone with a man called Simeon, talking about Julian the Apostate. The room was full of intimacy, still deep, like a pool.

> But Jacob moved. He murmured good-night. He went out into the court. He buttoned his jacket across his chest. He went back to his rooms, and being the only man who walked at the moment back to his rooms, his footsteps rang out. His figure loomed large. Back from the Chapel, back from the Hall, back from the Library, came the sound of his footsteps, as if the old stone echoed with magisterial authority. The young man—the young man—the young man—back to his rooms.

Now that is prose which uses every device of poetry save unbroken rhythm. It has rhythm, but it would not be as easy to arrange in *vers libre* as *A Haunted House*. The cadences are musical, but they are the music of prose. Sound and sense are allied. The plangent reiteration echoes the sound of footsteps. Mrs. Woolf has reached a combination of poetic and cinema technique which is almost wholly satisfying.

Chapter IV concerns the boating holiday when Jacob and Timmy Durrant go to Cornwall by way of the Scilly Isles. The first picture is a sea peace with the delicate sunlit colors of Russell Flint. The young men quarrel and enjoy themselves. There follows one of Mrs. Woolf's characteristic devices, a picture of the mainland from the sea.

> The mainland, not so very far off—you could see clefts in the cliffs, white cottages, smoke going up—wore an extraordinary look of calm, of sunny peace, as if wisdom and piety had descended upon the dwellers there. Now a cry sounded as of a man calling pilchards in a main street. It wore an extraordinary look of piety and peace, as if old men smoked by the door, and girls stood, hands on hips, at the well, and horses stood; as if the end of the world had come, and cabbage fields and stone walls and coastguard stations, and above all, the white sand bays with the waves breaking unseen by anyone, rose to heaven in a kind of ecstasy.
>
> But imperceptibly the cottage smoke droops, has the look of a mourning emblem, a flag floating its caress over a grave. The gulls, making their broad flight and then riding at peace, seem to mark the grave.
>
> No doubt if this were Italy, Greece, or even the shores of Spain, sadness would be routed by strangeness and excitement and the nudge of a classical education. But the Cornish hills have stark chimneys standing on them; and, somehow or other, loveliness is infernally sad. Yes, the chimneys and the coastguard stations and the little bays with waves breaking unseen by anyone make all remember the overpowering sorrow. And what can this sorrow be?
>
> It is brewed by the earth itself. It comes from the houses on the coast. We start transparent, then the cloud thickens. All history backs our pane of glass. To escape is vain.

Now that passage says a great many things. It gives a pictorial description of the Cornish coast. It hints by colloquial phrases, "loveliness is infernally sad," that the picture is seen by the young men from the boat. It hints by a remote reference to Shelley—"All history backs our pane of glass."—"A dome of many-coloured glass"?—that they are literary young men. It conveys an impression of melancholy which is a

common enough experience to persons of sensibility who look at land
from the detachment of the water, and it ends with a characteristic gesture
of debonair uncertainty: ''But whether this is the right interpretation of
Jacob's gloom as he sat naked, in the sun, looking at Land's End, it is
impossible to say; for he never spoke a word.''

The holiday continues. Mrs. Durrant, Tim's mother, one of those
old iron aristocrats admired by Mrs. Woolf, patronizes the cottager, Mrs.
Pascoe; Jacob and Tim join the house party; there is a dinner; there are
girls on the terrace, in the drawing room, in yellow and blue and silver
gauze, like a Whistler picture; Clara Durrant—a Meredithian heroine—
cuts grapes high on a ladder for Jacob to take back with him, and gives
her heart as well. We are left uncertain of his condition. There are
obscurities here. There is a joke about begonias which, after prolonged
contemplation, I am quite unable to fathom. But by this time the style is
growing easier.

Next, there is Jacob, settled in an eighteenth-century house in
Bloomsbury, going daily to an office, having acquired a friend with a
Wellington nose called Bonamy. It is a rather sober and sombre picture,
full of buses and clerks and a blind beggar woman in the London streets.
Then Jacob becomes Bohemian, and at a Guy Fawkes party on Parlia-
ment Hill?—somewhere certainly where the light from a bonfire can
show St. Paul's—he meets Florinda, who is a young woman not at all of
the type familiar to Clara Durrant, a young woman who lives a life of a
doubtful virtue, in a cheap mustard-colored bedroom, half attic, half
studio.

The Florinda chapters, with their irony and understanding, are
magnificent. They treat, of course, of sex. Florinda was, though in a
Chelseaesque and amateurish way, a prostitute; she ''caught'' the innocent Jacob, ready game for even so casual a huntress. But Mrs. Woolf is
not shocked. She is not solemn. She can, it appears, regard sex with
steady and amused comprehension. Florinda said she was a virgin, which
was doubtful. ''But whether or not she was a virgin seems a matter of no
importance whatever,'' says Mrs. Woolf, ''unless, indeed, it is the only
thing of any importance at all.'' Then, ironically, she draws her picture of
the London streets, with men and women seething up and down the
well-worn beats. ''Late homecomers could see shadows against the
blinds even in the most respectable suburbs. Not a square in snow or fog
lacked its amorous couple. All plays turned on the same subject; yet we
say it is a matter of no importance at all.

''If Florinda had a mind, she might have read with clearer eyes than
we can. She and her sort have solved the question by turning it into a trifle
of washing the hands nightly before going to bed, the only difficulty

being whether you prefer your water hot or cold, which being settled, the mind can go about its business unassailed.''

Now that, for a woman writing in 1922, was an unexpected attitude. It was the attitude of one who dared to regard sex with the same unalarmed detachment with which she regarded the coast of Cornwall. And with humor. Whatever the other Georgians thought about sex, they regarded it with solemnity. The disciples of D. H. Lawrence, James Joyce or Middleton Murry might smile at religion, and shrug their shoulders at sociology. But Sex is serious. It is as though they could never follow Mrs. Woolf's habit of pushing off in a boat from the mainland and regarding it dispassionately with detachment from the sea.

But Mrs. Woolf can. Even when Jacob finds that Florinda is faithless, and his disappointment turns London into a nightmare of squalor wherein the nightingales themselves are obscene, even then Mrs. Woolf remains objective, interested, a trifle amused. She employs her old trick of drawing all the external world, the streets and the lights and the voices, and a picture of the winter's night, bitterly cold in the frost outside, into her conspiracy to show how Jacob felt about Florinda. But she knew also that such feelings do not endure for long in healthy young men like Jacob Flanders.

He is a healthy young man. Though his conduct with Florinda is not at all of the kind likely to reassure his mother in Scarborough, writing letters with her toes on the fender, and hoping that all is well with the boy, it does not damage him. For when he emerges from his bedroom door, followed by Florinda yawning and arranging her hair, he comes ''in his dressinggown, amiable, authoritative, beautifully healthy like a baby after an airing, with an eye as clear as running water.'' As a necessary, interesting, but not overwhelmingly important episode in life, Mrs. Woolf puts sex in its place.

The whole Florinda episode is set into the proportion which Mrs. Woolf thinks fitting for it, partly by its companion picture of Clara Durrant's life, and partly by the first hint of coming catastrophe, which will blow to pieces this carefully constructed world.

While Jacob is consorting with Florinda, and later with Laurette and Fanny and Sandra Wentworth Williams, Clara Durrant, who loves him, leads the life of a debutante. She buys carnations; she attends the dressmaker; she introduces guests at her mother's parties; she practices a little mild philanthropy to the poor of Notting Hill and Clerkenwell. The same routine of social obligation which had bound Katharine Hilbery binds her. It frustrates her opportunity of knowing Jacob as it frustrates her opportunity of learning Italian or playing on the piano more than one sonata. Clara has not Katharine Hilbery's force of intellect or character, nor the raw intelligence of Rachel Vinrace, but she sometimes surprises observers by a strength of emotion which suggests something almost heroic in her character.

All this, however, is subordinated to the dressmakers and parties. Without a word of theorizing or protest, Mrs. Woolf suggests the contrast between the lives of young men and young women in prewar society. Jacob is so firm, so reticent, romantic, adventurous, passing from adventures of education to adventures of sex, and from these to adventures of travel and work and danger. Clara is so vague and shadowy and blushing, bending her pretty head over paper flowers, leaving calling-cards, driving to the Opera, weeping after proposals, a creature of hesitations, emotions, acquiescences, her only strength in love, and that doomed to frustration. Bonamy, Jacob's friend, could not help feeling compassion for her, even while he marveled at the insipidity of an "existence squeezed and emasculated within a white satin shoe."

That is one contrast. If Jacob knows disillusionment and ugliness, Clara never has any chance of knowing anything more than wishes unfulfilled. The pictures in which she appears are drawn always in the same soft, rosy colors, whereas Jacob's spin from violence of vivid light to darkness. It is Clara for whom one feels compassion, even after Jacob's moment of anguish in Soho, knowing that Florinda is false to him.

But contrasted with the picture from Clara's life is the foreboding of Jacob's coming death. Right in the middle of the Florinda episode Mrs. Woolf hints it. She shows us Rose Shaw talking to Mr. Bowley about a certain Jimmy who refused to marry a girl called Helen Aitken. . . . "And now Jimmy feeds crows in Flanders and Helen visits hospitals. Oh, life is damnable, life is wicked, as Rose Shaw said." That is all. A little, apparently irrelevant interpolation, a flash forward across some years; for this all takes place before the war. Yet it has been set there deliberately, perhaps to show us that life's anguish is made tolerable only when balanced by death.

Life may be wicked, but it is better than nonexistence; it is better than Clara Durrant's half-life. The pictures continue. They increase in brilliance and variety. Jacob recovers from Florinda, lunches with a countess, hunts in Essex, argues with Bonamy, takes tea with ladies, reads in the British Museum, goes to a party in Hammersmith and walks home afterwards feeling that life is good. He spends a reasonable evening with a prostitute called Laurette, and flutters the heart of an artist's model, Fanny Elmer. He goes to Paris, and finds that city and the people who live there more wonderful than anything in the world, for, in spite of his looks, his solidity and his reticence, he is still very young and naïve. He visits Italy; he visits Athens; he falls in love with an experienced married woman traveling with her bored politician husband; he accompanies them to Constantinople. He returns to London in the height of the season, his pockets full of Greek notes, giving no thought to Clara, Fanny or Florinda, though all three thought of him. Florinda was going to have a baby by Nick Bramham. The question of her virginity, then, was settled, and in the way least comfortable to herself. Sandra Wentworth Williams looked at her own little boy, and decided that Jacob, for all his good looks and solidity, was a small boy himself. But all the time, as Jacob sat in the Park, as Clara drove to the opera, as Florinda bargained with Nick Bramham in Verrey's, and Betty Flanders wrote her letters, the war was closing down on them.

Very quietly Mrs. Woolf conveys the impression of war, like fate, closing down upon her characters. There is first that hint of Jimmy killed and Helen visiting hospitals—no word of explanation why this should have happened. Nearly a hundred pages further on, as Mrs. Bowley is handing strawberries in the Durrants' drawing room, we are told, "The battleships ray out over the North Sea." Old General Gibbon asks, "Where are the men? . . . Where are the guns?" When Jacob returns from Greece, and sits in Hyde Park thinking of Sandra's letters, Clara, doomed to miss him, exercises her terrier and, with half her mind on Jacob, worries with the other half about her mother, who is much disturbed by the position of England. Mr. Bowley reassures her, "England's all right." But meanwhile a procession with banners passes down Whitehall. At the Admiralty news is received of the Reichstag. Clerks transmit rumors from Vienna; their faces grow grave as they write; Timmy Durrant is among the clerks. The Cabinet meets. "Sixteen gentlemen lifting their pens or turning perhaps wearily in their chairs, decreed that the course of history should shape itself this way." A placard is tied round a lamppost in Whitehall. " 'The Kaiser,' a far-away voice remarks, 'received me in audience.' " Out in Greece, where Jacob has been so recently, "the ships in the Piraeus fired their guns. The sound spread itself flat, and then went tunnelling its way with fitful explosions among the channels of the islands. Darkness drops like a knife over Greece."

> "The guns?" said Betty Flanders half asleep, getting out of bed and going to the window, which was decorated with a fringe of dark leaves. "Not at this distance," she thought. "It is the sea." Again, far away, she heard the dull sound, as if nocturnal women were beating great carpets. There was Morty lost, and Seabrook dead; her sons fighting for their Country. But were the chickens safe? Was that someone moving downstairs? Rebecca with the toothache? No. The nocturnal women were beating great carpets. Her hens shifted slightly on their perches.

There is only one more picture. Betty Flanders and Bonamy go to tidy up Jacob's room. " 'He left everything just as it was,' Bonamy marvelled. . . . 'What did he expect? Did he think he would come back?' "

It is clear that he will not come back. He has gone forever. His room, his bills, his letters, his invitations are all that remain, and his old shoes in the bedroom. The survivors must dispose somehow of these possessions, more durable than their owner. Jacob's room is empty, save for these. All the world has, indeed, been Jacob's room—Cornwall, Scarborough, London, Italy, Athens. Nothing remains now except what he has discarded. What has been lost? These have been lost to Jacob; Jacob has been lost to Bonamy and to his mother, to Clara and Fanny and Sandra. The possession and the loss are double. We dwell in ourselves; we dwell in the mirror that lies in the eyes of our friends regarding us. This, it would seem, is what this novel means.

As an accomplishment, it was something of a *tour de force*. It took literary England by storm. Here was something new, strange, beautiful. "It is authentic poetry, cognisant of the soul," said Rebecca West. "It is a novel in a thousand," said several others. It was, indeed, a triumphant experiment in a new technique.

But now that we can set it beside Mrs. Woolf's later work, beside *Mrs. Dalloway* and *To the Lighthouse* and *The Waves*, we know that it was not the best that she could do. The cinematograph style was brilliantly effective, but it was not as subtle as the orchestral effect which she was to use in *To the Lighthouse*; she was to obtain a surer control over her material in *Mrs. Dalloway*. She was to adventure further into obscure realms of human consciousness in *The Waves*. The contrasts, perhaps, in *Jacob's Room* are too violent. There are obscurities which even the most diligent study cannot penetrate. The effect created is very largely visual. Later she would plunge into the nerves, the brain, the senses of her characters, exploring further, yet binding the whole more closely into a unity of mood.

As for her sense of life, it shines vividly through every page, varied, exquisite, but not insipid. There runs, indeed, all through *Jacob's Room* a hint of cruelty: the crab tries to escape from the bucket; kind Mrs. Flanders smiles at Topaz; Jacob neglects Clara; Florinda has a baby by the wrong man; Sandra Wentworth Williams is heartless; Jacob dies.

The world, with all its beauty and adventure, its richness and variety, is darkened by cruelty. Death, if it ends the loveliness, the adventure, ends also that. Death balances the picture. It completes the pattern. It makes even cruelty fall into place. It is completion.

Virginia Woolf

Introduction to Mrs. Dalloway

It is difficult—perhaps impossible—for a writer to say anything about his own work. All he has to say has been said as fully and as well as he can in the body of the book itself. If he has failed to make his meaning clear there it is scarcely likely that he will succeed in some few pages of preface or postscript. And the author's mind has another peculiarity which is also hostile to introductions. It is as inhospitable to its offspring as the hen sparrow is to hers. Once the young birds can fly, fly they must; and by the time they have fluttered out of the nest the mother bird has begun to think perhaps of another brood. In the same way once a book is printed and published it ceases to be the property of the author; he commits it to the care of other people; all his attention is claimed by some new book which not only thrusts its predecessor from the nest but has a way of subtly blackening its character in comparison with its own.

It is true that the author can if he wishes tell us something about himself and his life which is not in the novel; and to this effort we should do all that we can to encourage him. For nothing is more fascinating than to be shown the truth which lies behind those immense façades of fiction—if life is indeed true, and if fiction is indeed fictitious. And probably the connection between the two is highly complicated. Books are the flowers or fruit stuck here and there on a tree which has its roots deep down in the earth of our earliest life, of our first experiences. But here again to tell the reader anything that his own imagination and insight have not already discovered would need not a page or two of preface but a

From Mrs. Dalloway, *by Virginia Woolf, Modern Library edition, 1928. Copyright 1928. Reprinted by permission of Random House, Inc.*

35

volume or two of autobiography. Slowly and cautiously one would have to go to work, uncovering, laying bare, and even so when everything had been brought to the surface, it would still be for the reader to decide what was relevant and what not. Of *Mrs. Dalloway* then one can only bring to light at the moment a few scraps, of little importance or none perhaps; as that in the first version Septimus, who later is intended to be her double, had no existence; and that Mrs. Dalloway was originally to kill herself, or perhaps merely to die at the end of the party. Such scraps are offered humbly to the reader in the hope that like other odds and ends they may come in useful.

But if one has too much respect for the reader pure and simple to point out to him what he has missed, or to suggest to him what he should seek, one may speak more explicitly to the reader who has put off his innocence and become a critic. For though criticism, whether praise or blame, should be accepted in silence as the legitimate comment which the act of publication invites, now and again a statement is made without bearing on the book's merits or demerits which the writer happens to know to be mistaken. One such statement has been made sufficiently often about *Mrs. Dalloway* to be worth perhaps a word of contradiction. The book, it was said, was the deliberate offspring of a method. The author, it was said, dissatisfied with the form of fiction then in vogue, was determined to beg, borrow, steal or even create another of her own. But, as far as it is possible to be honest about the mysterious process of the mind, the facts are otherwise. Dissatisfied the writer may have been; but her dissatisfaction was primarily with nature for giving an idea, without providing a house for it to live in. The novelists of the preceding generation had done little—after all why should they?—to help. The novel was the obvious lodging, but the novel it seemed was built on the wrong plan. Thus rebuked the idea started as the oyster starts or the snail to secrete a house for itself. And this it did without any conscious direction. The little note book in which an attempt was made to forecast a plan was soon abandoned, and the book grew day by day, week by week, without any plan at all, except that which was dictated each morning in the act of writing. The other way, to make a house and then inhabit it, to develop a theory and then apply it, as Wordsworth did and Coleridge, is, it need not be said, equally good and much more philosophic. But in the present case it was necessary to write the book first and to invent a theory afterwards.

If, however, one singles out the particular point of the book's methods for discussion it is for the reason given—that it has been made the subject of comment by critics, not that in itself it deserves notice. On the contrary, the more successful the method, the less it attracts attention.

The reader it is to be hoped will not give a thought to the book's method or to the book's lack of method. He is concerned only with the effect of the book as a whole on his mind. Of that most important question he is a far better judge than the writer. Indeed, given time and liberty to frame his own opinion he is eventually an infallible judge. To him then the writer commends *Mrs. Dalloway* and leaves the court confident that the verdict whether for instant death or for some years more of life and liberty will in either case be just.

Lucio P. Ruotolo

Clarissa Dalloway

One October afternoon in 1929 Virginia Woolf was grasped by "inner loneliness" on the streets of London. Later that day, when considering this moment of "vacancy and silence," she recalled a similar emotion following her brother's death twenty years earlier. Her diary, however, reveals an important difference: "No one knows how I suffer, walking up this street, engaged with my anguish, as I was after Thoby died—alone; fighting something alone. But then I had the devil to fight, and now nothing." While failing to understand the disruptive feeling, she confesses that it has goaded her to reach beyond the habitable world. Virginia Woolf equates this "emptiness" with a new and no less obscure impression of freedom, "the sense that comes to me of being bound on an adventure; of being strangely free now, with money and so on, to do anything."[1]

A few months before her painful rejuvenation in the face of nothing, Martin Heidegger, appointed to the chair of philosophy at Freiburg, delivered his inaugural lecture on the primacy of such an experience. Heidegger's assertion that man must face nothing in order to be something, and Virginia Woolf's literary treatment of the dilemma she acknowledged in her own life, characterize the ontological reformation that with Schelling and Kierkegaard had begun to transform Western culture.[2]

[1] *A Writer's Diary,* Leonard Woolf ed. (New York: Harcourt, Brace, 1954) p. 144.

[2] For a good discussion of the historical background of this ontological shift, particularly the pre-Socratic Parmenides, see Paul Tillich's "Being and Nonbeing," *Systematic Theology,* vol. I (Chicago: University of Chicago Press, 1967), pp. 186–189. See also William Barrett, *Irrational Man* (New York: Doubleday, 1958), pp. 102–103.

The critical moment of absolute doubt, while symptomatic of the recurrent madness that plagued Virginia Woolf throughout her life, is a central concern of her most creative work. Rachel, the earliest of her heroines (*The Voyage Out*), is overcome by "the unspeakable queerness of the fact that she should be sitting in an arm-chair, in the morning, in the middle of the world" or "that things should exist at all." When Eleanor (*The Years*) questions her place in the world, she is gripped by the anxious sense of being "alone in the midst of nothingness." Louis (*The Waves*) directs his friends to the sound of the world "moving through abysses of infinite space," a blank and timeless reality that dissolves identity. The theme is expressed in *Mrs. Dalloway* when Septimus Smith, gazing at England from the window of a train, ponders that "the world itself is without meaning."[3] Virginia Woolf, in both critical essays and fiction, pictures man's acknowledgment of an absurd universe. Her chief artistic concern is to explore the nature of that intelligence capable of surviving negation.

"Mr. Bennett and Mrs. Brown," a lecture she gave at Cambridge in 1924 while working on *Mrs. Dalloway,* raises the question of how and why a character appears real. Woolf, like Heidegger, asks, What is Being?[4] Both novelist and philosopher charge their contemporaries with uncritically accepting society's concept of reality. Virginia Woolf speaks of her age as defining "old women" through the predictable associations that make them discernible in the first place: "Old women have houses. They have fathers. They have incomes. They have servants. They have hot-water bottles. That is how we know that they are old women."[5] She censures the preceding Edwardians for their presumption that any sensible man knows the difference between what is and what is not. In her novels the heroes' function is to examine critically the existential relevance of their own lives. Significantly, meaning is revealed to these heroes when its antithesis becomes more than a matter of sophistry. Her lecture, later published in *The Captain's Death Bed,* offers "Mrs. Brown" as a touchstone for the virtue that is to characterize her most famous protagonists.

---

[3] Virginia Woolf, *Mrs. Dalloway* (New York: Harcourt, Brace, 1925), p. 133, copyright, 1925, by Virginia Woolf; renewed 1953, by Leonard Woolf. Reprinted by permission of Harcourt Brace Jovanovich, Inc., the author's literary estate, and the Hogarth Press. All page references are to this edition.

[4] While in this particular essay Virginia Woolf is dealing with the novelist's effort to portray character, her concern with that which makes a character seem real in fiction presumes and confronts a larger horizon of experienced reality.

[5] Virginia Woolf, *The Captain's Death Bed* (New York: Harcourt, Brace, 1950), p. 113. All page references are to this edition. The first version of her essay appeared in print in *Nation & Athenaeum,* December 1, 1923. The title of her Cambridge lecture was "Character and Fiction."

Mrs. Brown is a fictitious name for an old woman the lecturer once saw on a train to London. Virginia Woolf recalls that as she sat opposite the stranger, Mrs. Brown was in the midst of a serious talk with her companion, a stern-faced man of about forty (he is given the effectively impersonal name of Smith); it was apparent to the intruder that the latter had some power over the former "which he was exerting disagreeably" (p. 99). Since they stopped their discussion in her presence, she remains ignorant as to the cause of the woman's suffering.

At first the novelist confesses the desire "like most people traveling with fellow passengers" somehow to account for them, and so she conceives the familiar details through which these unknown people might be established as more legible characters. The woman, she imagines, widowed years ago, has one son who is in some sort of trouble; her tormentor, dressed in good blue serge, is "very likely a respectable cornchandler from the North" (p. 98).

When they begin speaking again, the small talk that Mr. Smith initiates with composed condescension verifies the power he holds over the little woman by his side. As the latter attempts to keep up the appearance of civility, resisting all of his menacing, though unspoken, demands, Virginia Woolf is suddenly aware of a superb dignity in Mrs. Brown's struggle to preserve the sanctity of her being against an overbearing and callous adversary: "She looked very small, very tenacious; at once very frail and very heroic." The lecturer recalls how at that moment a mysterious sense of Mrs. Brown's existence seemed to flow across the empty space of the compartment, disturbing her with an excitement that (like the experience of dread on the streets of London) she cannot fully understand. The impression the old lady made, Virginia Woolf tells us, "was overwhelming. It came pouring out like a draught, like a smell of burning" (pp. 100–101). All the facts packed into a three-volume novel of Mrs. Brown (and the traveler was tempted to write one) cannot improve upon this obscurely defined sense of recognition.

The Proustian manner in which Mrs. Brown's heroism appears to the novelist resists her effort to conceptualize the experience. Bothered by a sense of obscurity, Virginia Woolf turns to such eminent Edwardian novelists as H. G. Wells, John Galsworthy, and Arnold Bennett to study the way in which they communicated phenomena. Wells's utopian considerations, Galsworthy's social criticism, and Bennett's aesthetic predilection (she argues that Bennett tries "to hypnotize us into the belief that, because he has made a house, there must be a person living there") presume the bond between reader and writer to be a common way of seeing and ordering experience, exemplified by the age's habit of describing old women. In each case it is not the particular existence of a

Mrs. Brown that is the starting point for communication; rather, Virginia Woolf insists, these writers "were interested in something outside," and the nature of their respective ideologies determined their manner of seeing. For the Edwardian, essence preceded existence. Virginia Woolf suggests that her contemporaries have largely ignored the particularity of human existence: "With all his powers of observation, . . . Mr. Bennett has never once looked at Mrs. Brown in her corner" (p. 109).

Rather than censure the conventions which writers such as Arnold Bennett have utilized and developed, the novelist argues that changing times have rendered their ways obsolete: "For us those conventions are ruin, those tools are death" (p. 110). She seeks an idiom more in tune with the artistic and scientific break-throughs that have characterized the new century.

Mrs. Brown's presence dissipates the novelist's Edwardian frame of reference: "Details could wait. The important thing was to realize her character, to steep oneself in her atmosphere" (p. 101). The statement appears to assert the strange proposition that human personality is manifest in atmosphere rather than in substance. Virginia Woolf enunciates the emptiness that surrounds and separates people; space becomes her catalyst for communication. The idea is similar to Heidegger's formulation throughout *Being and Time* of that enveloping space within which "presence" is revealed.[6]

William Barrett, recalling Buber's I-Thou concept, suggests that "for Heidegger, the I can meet the Thou only because *There is*—i.e., can meet only within some encompassing region of Being. After all, I have to meet thee *somewhere;* in relation to something and in some context." Barrett considers the emphasis upon this "third presence," the region where subject and object can meet, as Heidegger's most important philosophical insight.[7]

Heidegger's concept of Being plunges all phenomenological experience into the uncertainty of a future that is yet to be and a past that is irredeemably over. The inauthentic man, unwilling to risk the void that borders meaning, maintains a static vision of existence. Only in nothingness, Heidegger stresses, lies the possibility for the emergence of a world that is more than the projection of derived intentions.

Utilizing her dramatic example, Virginia Woolf urges the modern writer to face a human dimension that both underlies and transcends "the fabric of things," to look beneath conventional behavior into a private

---

[6]For an analysis of Heidegger's meaning here see William Barrett, *What Is Existentialism?* (New York: Grove Press, 1964), pp. 161, 185, and Magda King, *Heidegger's Philosophy* (New York: Macmillan, 1964), pp. 5–33.

[7]*What Is Existentialism?*, pp. 141, 193.

world each of us possesses. The "world" she has in mind is radically different from that of her predecessors. It is a world in which impermanence and paradox ridicule bourgeois complacency, in which "you have gone to bed at night bewildered by the complexity of your feelings. In one day thousands of ideas have coursed through your brains; thousands of emotions have met, collided, and disappeared in astonishing disorder" (p. 118).

The threat of meaninglessness leads her to that same sense of creative possibility she was to describe in her diary. The old woman, existing in an atmosphere of "unlimited capacity and infinite variety," is free to say and do the unexpected. Everything about her, not least of all her silence, fascinates the writer for the reason expressed at the close of her essay: "She is, of course, the spirit we live by, life itself" (p. 119). The details of her face, her gestures, the quality of her speech, have emerged in a new light once the novelist has shared Mrs. Brown's crisis. Virginia Woolf's closing advice that English literature will reach a new greatness only "if we are determined never, never to desert Mrs. Brown"—like the axiom of phenomenology, *"Zu den Sachen selbst!"* ("To the things themselves!")—urges her contemporaries to tunnel with her into the depth of life and character, in search of what Husserl termed the "genesis of meaning" (*Sinngenesis*).[8]

Mrs. Dalloway opposes the Edwardians' unwillingness to question their order; it also represents Virginia Woolf's effort to establish a perspective for the novel outside the realm of manners. The book, written several years before she recorded her suffering on the streets of London, like Heidegger's now classic study, explores nothingness within the context of Being and time.

Virginia Woolf in an early preface describes Septimus and Clarissa as doubles. Initially, the parallel seems obscure. Clarissa, a fashionable Edwardian matron, entrenched in the establishment of British society, lives within the bounds she has freely chosen. Above all she affirms with aristocratic fervor that particularly English virtue, the right to privacy. Septimus, returning from the war, a victim of shell shock (it is the summer of 1923), wanders with his Italian bride through an environment without form or function; only his consciousness qualifies absurdity. He likens himself to a half-drowned sailor, marooned on an uncharted rock

---

[8]Note Harvena Richter's discussion of the original working plan for *The Waves:* "The novel is visualized as a poetic-encyclopedic reconstruction of the creation and development of man and his mind, moving from his earliest awareness of objects—'the beginning with pure sensations,' Mrs. Woolf noted in an early outline of part one—to a perception of the world, death, and time." *Virginia Woolf: The Inward Voyage* (Princeton, N.J.: Princeton University Press, 1970), p. 80.

in the midst of some nameless ocean. The novel pictures twelve hours in the lives of these two people, Clarissa preparing for one of her grand parties, Septimus in his private dialogue with cosmic anarchy. Although the two never meet, as the novelist develops her characters we realize they share a common insight through their experience of nothingness.

Clarissa's respect for the distance between human beings, more than a manifestation of detached decorum, leads her to defend Septimus' suicide when she hears of it late that evening. Her identification with Septimus is not a detail derived from those activities that describe Clarissa's life as a wealthy London matron. Indeed, the people closest to the heroine, bound by the conventions that define their social station, have the greatest difficulty perceiving her.

Mrs. Dalloway is more than casually concerned with the way in which people see. The world of Clarissa, her double, and her former fiancé, Peter Walsh, takes on a novel and frightening appearance once stripped of its predefined context. "Things," Peter confesses after his disturbing interview with Clarissa, "stand out as if one had never seen them before" (p. 107). Similarly, Peter's presence in her house after years of absence makes Clarissa see herself in a new way.

Peter finds that the sight of her elicits an ambiguous response. He is at once drawn to Clarissa as a reminder of past affection and repulsed by the anxiety her presence occasions. When such encounters threaten his composure, he seeks respite through the habit and affectation that pre-define him—the fondling of his penknife or his predictably romantic invective against Edwardian decorum. Virginia Woolf stresses Peter's compulsion for self-distraction during his fantasy in the park, when, like the young Stephen Dedalus before the Dublin prostitute, he urges the vision to grant him the peace of non-being: "Let me walk straight on to this great figure, who will, with a toss of her head, mount me on her streamers and let me blow to nothingness with the rest" (p. 87).

The irony of the Edwardians' remedy for insanity is implicit in Dr. Holmes's instructions for Septimus' wife to force her husband to take notice of "real things." Each of Rezia's pleas for Septimus to look at details elicits his despair over the world that others would foist upon him: "But what was there to look at?" (p. 37).

Rezia, we are told, could not help looking at detail. When the motor car moves through the streets of London arousing so much speculation as to the identity of the dignitary behind the curtained window, her attention is riveted upon the pattern of trees on the blinds. Like the silks and feathers of the hats she manufactures, such details fully absorb her. Dr. Holmes easily converts Rezia to the therapy of making Septimus "take an interest in things outside himself" (p. 31). His prescription typifies the inauthenticity that touches every character in the novel. Rezia is forever concerned with what other people will think of her husband's odd behavior. Richard Dalloway is reminded that he loves his wife when he recalls that Peter Walsh once loved her. Clarissa gives parties so people will like her. About these central characters float a chorus of sleep-walkers, the countless passersby shaken into momentary consciousness by the backfiring of an automobile, merging with a crowd of onlookers before an airplane skywriting advertisements, seeking self-distraction in every object. Was the plane spelling toffee or soap? Was it the Prince of Wales or the Prime Minister whose face was seen in the passing car? What flowers to choose for the party? The man on the street, like Prufrock considering peaches and trouser cuffs, avoids the question that over-whelms Septimus.

Septimus' vision of the world alienates him from the objective order wife and psychiatrist urge him to emulate. Estranged from the sanity of others, "rooted to the pavement," the veteran asks "for what purpose" he is present. Virginia Woolf's novel honors and extends his ques-tion. He perceives a beauty in existence that his age has almost totally disregarded; his vision of new life—"Trees were alive" (p. 32)—is a source of joy as well as of madness. These obscure words, scribbled on pieces of paper, recall Wordsworth's critique of a world intent upon "getting and spending," out of touch with Being. Unfortu-nately, the glimpse of beauty that makes Septimus less forlorn is anathema to an age that worships like Septimus' inhuman doctor, Sir William Bradshaw, the twin goddesses "Proportion" and "Conver-sion" (pp. 150–151).

While the average inhabitant of London discourses on the commer-cial products advertised in the sky, Septimus is moved to tears by them: "the smoke words languishing and melting in the sky . . . one shape after another of unimaginable beauty" (p. 31). He participates in the presence of all he perceives (animate and inanimate alike). If the leaves themselves appear alive, they are connected "by millions of fibres with his own body" (p. 32), just as sparrows rising and falling between a host of objects are all part of the pattern. "Sounds made harmonies with premeditation; the spaces between them were as significant as the sounds" (p. 33). Septimus, however, terrified by his eccentric vision, remains isolated from the everyday world.

Septimus and Clarissa realize detail each in a different way. When Septimus lies back in his chair, exhausted with fear, his body is suddenly thrilled by the sense of the earth beneath him. In exuberation he imagines that "red flowers grew through his flesh" (p. 103), their stiff leaves rustling by his head. During the fantasy, the flowers become roses that hang about him; it is only then that the vision reveals its source: his bedroom is wallpapered with thick red roses. The starting place for Septimus' consciousness is generally a point that transcends the object that has occasioned speculation. As a result, he lacks an existential center from which to project his vision of the present into the future. The realization that he is responsible for holding together a vision that threatens momentarily to burst into meaninglessness fills him with terror. "It is I," Septimus confesses in anxiety, "who am blocking the way" (p. 21). The frightening discrepancy between his own experience and the static world toward which his community urges him tempts Septimus to hope that the latter will supply stability. Like Lear in the wilderness, "He would not go mad." Ironically, his attempt to preserve sanity leads him at times to deny the very vision of chaos that distinguishes him from the crowd.

While Clarissa appears bound by the decorum from which Septimus flees, the opening pages of the novel reveal her more affirmative impulses.[9] Virginia Woolf uses the appropriate image of a bird to describe the expansive manner in which Mrs. Dalloway's thoughts take flight from detail. There is, as one of her neighbors describes Clarissa, "a touch of the bird about her" (p. 4). The squeak of hinges and an open door recall the freedom of her youth when the air seemed open. On the London curb she appears "perched," as if in expectation of flight from the confining aspects of practical considerations. While the fact that she must buy flowers for the party motivates her trip to the florist and remains an important concern, she allows the object—flowers—the possibility of opening up a host of other visual connotations. "Things," animated by her presence, are given new life through a complex of intentions far greater than the concern of utility.

Clarissa does not close her eyes once she acknowledges the startling disparity between existential and practical detail; rather she possesses the resiliency to move back and forth between these contrary visions of the world. The booming sounds of Big Ben, the noise of traffic, the prattle of shoppers, through Clarissa's presence are all transformed without loss of their reference in objective time and space. "Heaven only knows why one loves it so," Clarissa speculates while crossing Victoria Street, "how one sees it so, making it up, building it round one, tumbling it, creating it every moment afresh" (p. 5). What she loved, Virginia Woolf assures us, was London on this particular moment of a June morning.

[9]Geoffrey H. Hartman speaks of "the affirmative impulse" in Virginia Woolf's critique of world as a quality of the artist that points dialectically beyond itself. *Beyond Formalism* (New Haven, Conn.: Yale University Press, 1970), p. 74.

As Clarissa and Septimus stand in separate places on the streets of London, they respond creatively to similar detail: the backfiring of a car, the passing crowds, an airplane skywriting advertisements. Both characters likewise acknowledge an accompanying sense of dread. The unpredictable quality of Being fills the protagonist with a disturbing "solemnity," (the word recurs continually in these opening pages) as if, she first tells us when gazing out the window, "something awful was about to happen" (p. 3). It is the same feeling she acknowledges in that pause before Big Ben strikes, the sense of wonder that we should be at all, that clocks should be striking and that one should be standing there, loving and fearing such phenomena.

Clarissa allows things to reveal themselves in new ways once she has classified them within their familiar context. Her openness to innovation reflects her own independence. She does not require others to supply the meaning of her life. Her critique of "love" and "religion" is essentially an attack upon those who, under the sanction of passion or doctrine, presume to create others in their own image.

Doris Kilman (the name is apt), a Christian convert who serves as tutor to Clarissa's daughter, represents doctrinaire intolerance. Staking her claim in other people, she invades the lonely and mysterious "privacy of the soul" (p. 192). Clarissa finds Miss Kilman difficult because she utilizes others almost exclusively to mirror her own suffering.

People, like things, serve the characters of *Mrs. Dalloway* as means of sustaining their image of themselves. Even the heroine is tempted to make use of others to justify herself. The thought of the tutor's domination of her daughter, arousing Clarissa's feelings to a pitch of hatred, proves a distraction from the recurring sense of emptiness. "Kilman her enemy. That was satisfying; that was real. . . . It was enemies one wanted, not friends" (pp. 265–266). Friends require love, enemies sustain self-love; Clarissa describes her hatred as an expression of the latter. Contrary to her characteristic refusal to label other people or herself—"she would not say of herself, I am this, I am that" (p. 11)—she has created a definitive posture through an act of imposition. Like Peter and Miss Kilman she has chosen a self that relies upon the object of its passion. "Nobody . . . was more dependent upon others" (p. 241), Virginia Woolf suggests through Mrs. Dalloway, than Peter, whose tirades against English society cannot hide his need for recognition.

The objects that fill Clarissa with a *joie de vivre* are largely unnoticed by Peter, who is preoccupied with such general conceptions as "the state of the world . . . Wagner, Pope's poetry, people's characters eternally, and the defects of her own soul" (p. 9). The Hugh Whitbreads and the Lady Brutons of Mrs. Dalloway's world are genuinely lost in the details of writing letters to the *Times* and stocking the royal wine cellar; Peter and Clarissa's old friend Sally Seton oppose such lifeless conformity to outdated traditions with romantic invective. Like Miss Kilman and the psychiatrist Bradshaw, whose dogma drives Septimus to his death, their aim is to replace one orthodoxy with another. It is not by chance that the free and rebellious Sally should choose finally to marry a wealthy landowner and settle in on the Rosseter estate while Peter joins the Major Blimps in India.

For Clarissa, marriage like life must supply space for difference and for license; "a little independence there must be between people living together day in day out in the same house" (p. 10), a letting be that with Peter was always impossible. Peter, lacking "the ghost of a notion what anyone else was feeling" (p. 69), demanded to share everything and gave nothing out of fear of risking his "point of view." Clarissa finds such love intolerable.

Richard Dalloway, ignorant of his wife's motives, bumbling in his effort to communicate his affection to her, respects, as Peter cannot, the vacant silence that allows relationship: "there is a dignity in people; a solitude; even between husband and wife a gulf; and that one must respect, thought Clarissa, watching him [Richard] open the door; for one would not part with it oneself, or take it, against his will, from one's husband, without losing one's independence, one's self respect—" (p. 181). Even Richard, however, causes his wife unhappiness through misinterpreting her passion to entertain.

Both her husband and former fiancé "laughed at her very unjustly, for her parties" (p. 183); but this desire to give parties "for no reason whatever," which Peter felt was motivated by snobbery and Richard by foolishness expresses Clarissa's innermost love of Being as well as her inauthenticity; her parties are "an offering" to life itself. While confessing that her sense of offerings sounds "horribly vague," Virginia Woolf contrasts the heroine's commitment to others with the snobbish reserve of Edwardian society. It is the recognition of and respect for people—"she felt quite continuously a sense of their existence"—that inspires the heroine to bring them together. Clarissa's effort to reach "this thing she called life" (p. 184), leads her to acknowledge that the practical world cannot sustain her sense of mystery and significance, that every offering moves relentlessly toward its own annihilation. Clarissa's existential openness leads her continually to consider non-Being.

Significantly, Septimus' affirmation of life denies validity to its alternative: the birds in the trees sing to him that "there is no death" (p. 36). The most terrifying hallucination his madness must endure is the mirage of the deceased Evans, "for he could not look upon the dead" (p.

105). This self-deception enhances Septimus' isolation from others. Solipsism shelters him from the external evidence that life is linked with death. Like Sartre's prisoner in "The Wall," he seeks to sustain the illusion of being immortal in a world sheltered from human relationships. But his insanity is less rooted in the eccentric character of his perceptiveness than in the repression of that meaninglessness which typifies the times. His madness mirrors the crowd's compulsive pursuit of self-distraction. Septimus loses himself in a world of romantic introspection; the Bradshaws, avoiding the abyss of inwardness, seek through science and social hierarchy to bridle those untoward premonitions that emerge from the depths of human personality.

Mrs. Dalloway, who cannot bear the subject of death to be mentioned at her party, is no less a child of her age. Like the characters in Edward Albee's play named after Virginia Woolf, the heroine often transposes her anxieties into merriment, in this case into the poeticism of a line from *Cymbeline*. "Fear no more the heat o' the sun," like the singsong lyrics "Who's afraid of Virginia Woolf," serve to relieve the sense of life's absurd conclusion. In so doing, however, Clarissa experiences the frightening loss of her own personal being: "Often now this body she wore . . . this body, with all its capacities, seemed nothing—nothing at all. She had the oddest sense of being herself invisible; unseen; unknown . . . this being Mrs. Dalloway; not even Clarissa any more" (p. 14). As we have seen, such disruptive experiences enrich the heroine's relationship to her world. The sound of Big Ben striking, her Irish cook whistling in the kitchen, or Mr. Dalloway reading the *Times* at breakfast, stand out as "exquisite moments" because they exist tentatively against a backdrop of meaninglessness, against Clarissa's premonition "that it was very, very dangerous to live even one day" (p. 11).

Virginia Woolf explores the manner in which moments of Being come into focus through the awareness of its antithesis at several points in her book.[10] Employing the simile of a fading rocket to convey Rezia's feeling of alienation, she suggests that "the outline of houses and towers" as well as the surrounding countryside, menaced by darkness, exist again "more ponderously" than before: "I am alone; I am alone! she cried, . . . as perhaps at midnight, when all boundaries are lost, the country reverts to its ancient shape, as the Romans saw it, lying cloudy, when they landed, and the hills had no names and rivers wound they knew not where—such was her darkness" (pp. 34–35). Similarly, when Peter Walsh feels threatened by Clarissa's affection, the inanimate objects that fill his hotel room disclose new aspects of significance. "Any number of

---

[10]For a good discussion of the moment as a microcosm of Being in Virginia Woolf's writing, see Richter's *Virginia Woolf*, p. 40.

people had hung up their hats on those pegs. Even the flies, if you thought of it, had settled on other people's noses" (p. 235). More often than not the characters in Virginia Woolf's fictional world retreat before such moments of liberated perspective.

Where Peter and Rezia choose the passive luxury of self-pity, Clarissa, "like a nun withdrawing" from thoughts of life and death, seeks distraction reading memoirs or sewing. In the privacy of an empty room, reading Baron Marbot's description of the retreat from Moscow, Clarissa "could not dispel a virginity preserved through childbirth which clung to her like a sheet." This "emptiness about the heart of life; an attic room" (p. 45), threatens the heroine; it tempts her, as it does Peter, to submerge into oblivion. At other times, in the rising and falling of her needle and thread, she metaphorically commits the burden of her consciousness "to some sea, which sighs collectively for all sorrows, and renews, begins, collects, lets fall" (p. 59).

Clarissa, however, does not sanctify these withdrawals. When called back to the world by particular sounds—the ringing of the door bell while sewing, the sound of Richard opening a door when reading—she greets such interruptions with the enthusiasm that characterizes her openness to life. Lying awake, on her narrow bed, unable to sleep, she hears below "the click of the handle released as gently as possible by Richard, who slipped upstairs in his socks and then, as often as not, dropped his hot-water bottle and swore! How she laughed!" (p. 47).

From the emptiness of solitude Clarissa gains a new relationship to external phenomena. The most important vision that intrudes upon her is that of an old lady she has often seen through the parlor window. Clarissa's response to this unknown woman, framed in the window of an adjoining house like some archetypal inhabitant from a world unrealized, recalls Virginia Woolf's awe before the presence of Mrs. Brown. The encounter occurs twice in the course of the novel.

The old lady is first mentioned in contrast to Doris Kilman. As Clarissa looks across the space that separates the two buildings, her thoughts pursue Miss Kilman's unwillingness to let others be themselves. As if in benediction, she blesses the old lady's unfettered movements across the way: "Let her climb upstairs if she wanted to; let her stop; then let her, as Clarissa had often seen her, gain her bedroom, part her curtains, and disappear again into the background" (p. 191).

The old lady's activity is all the more extraordinary to Clarissa because it appears to follow the sounds of Big Ben striking the half hour. Through her movements the finger of time descended "down, into the midst of ordinary things . . . making the moment solemn." Like Mrs. Brown's gestures, which offer few particulars upon which to construct her history, the neighbor's motions reveal few descriptive facts. In life and art, however, such details are of secondary importance. "Why creeds and prayers and mackintoshes? when, thought Clarissa, that's the miracle, that's the mystery; that old lady" (p. 193).

The ability to see and to wonder at the existence of another human being may appear to be a somewhat obvious virtue. And yet sometime between September 1929 and December 1930, Ludwig Wittgenstein, during his only public lecture at Cambridge, given to the same small group of "Heretics" before which the novelist read her paper on "Mrs. Brown," felt called upon to emphasize for his learned audience the distinction between "the scientific way of looking at a fact," and "the experience of seeing the world as a miracle"; he equates the latter with "wondering at the existence of the world."[11] It is tempting to speculate that Virginia Woolf, who met the philosopher a number of times, might have heard about Wittgenstein's lecture.[12] Regardless of their possible communication, Woolf and Wittgenstein were aware of the complexity involved in their distinction and both felt called upon to make it.

Mrs. Dalloway expresses its author's distaste for the doctrinaire assumptions of an age bent on "solutions." With a fine touch of satire, the novelist describes Bradshaw—a patron of the arts—stopping to scrutinize one of the Dalloways' etchings: "He looked in the corner for the engraver's name" (p. 294). The famous psychiatrist worships, as we have seen, a formidable deity: "Conversion is her name and she feasts on the wills of the weakly, loving to impress , to impose, adoring her own features stamped on the face of the populace" (p. 151). As with Mr. Smith on the train to London, Bradshaw's strength relies upon the weakness of others. The hostess reveals upon seeing him later in the evening: "One wouldn't like Sir William to see one unhappy" (p. 278).

No doctrine of religion or love could hope to solve the "supreme mystery" that grasps Clarissa before the parlor window. The mystery which Miss Kilman or Peter might say they had solved, "but Clarissa didn't believe either of them had the ghost of an idea of solving, was simply this: here was one room; there another" (p. 193). As Heidegger stressed in his inaugural lecture, the important consideration about Being is not "what" or "how" it is, but rather "that" it is, and that one stands miraculously separated from another by a nowhere, by a gulf of nothing.[13]

[11]"Wittgenstein's Lecture on Ethics," *The Philosophical Review,* 74 (1965), 8–11.

[12]In a letter dated July 28, 1965, Leonard Woolf informs me that although he and his wife did not know Wittgenstein well they spent some time with him when the philosopher stayed with Maynard Keynes in a house close to their own.

[13]Martin Heidegger, "What Is Metaphysics?" *Existence and Being* (Chicago: Henry Regnery, 1949), pp. 325–361.

At the time of this first encounter with the old woman, Mrs. Dalloway is essentially a spectator. Her existential involvement occurs later at the height of her party when the hostess overhears Dr. Bradshaw talking about the suicide of a young patient (Septimus). With the intrusion of that forbidden subject—"Oh! thought Clarissa, in the middle of my party, here's death" (p. 279)—she withdraws in panic into a little room which the Prime Minister has just left. The chamber is empty, with only an impress upon the chairs to record that moment of history. "Alone in her finery," with neither guests nor routine to distract her, Mrs. Dalloway's crisis begins.

Significantly, the heroine's effort to face death recalls Virginia Woolf's temptation to account for the reality of Mrs. Brown within a fabric of details. Clarissa first strives to understand the young man's suicide through a context of factual description. "He had thrown himself from a window. Up had flashed the ground; through him, blundering, bruising, went the rusty spikes. There he lay with a thud, thud, thud in his brain, and then a suffocation of blackness. So she saw it." But the details of the tragedy prompt her to consider: "Why had he done it? And the Bradshaws talked of it at her party!" There follows an interesting shift as Clarissa apparently reverses the meaning of "it": "She had once thrown a shilling into the Serpentine, never anything more. But he had flung it away." Both life and death are bound indistinguishably in the impersonal pronoun, one as obscure as the other; what has Septimus lost and to what must Clarissa return? ("She would have to go back; the rooms were still crowded; people kept on coming.") The question of death not only has led the heroine to the question of life but has confused the two, recalling Heidegger's presupposition that Being and non-Being are inseparable. In the midst of this confusion, she establishes a meaning that redeems Septimus' obscure action: "A thing there was that mattered; a thing, wreathed about with chatter, defaced, obscured in her own life, let drop every day in corruption, lies, chatter. This he had preserved. Death was defiance. Death was an attempt to communicate" (p. 280).[14]

Clarissa (echoing the novelist's experience with Mrs. Brown) identifies herself with a human being attempting to preserve the sanctity of his soul from all who seek to control it. In so doing, however, she accepts, as Septimus cannot, the dread of holding the power of life and death in her own hands: "There was the terror; the overwhelming incapacity, one's parents giving it into one's hands, this life, to be lived to the end, to be walked with serenely; there was in the depths of her heart an awful fear" (p. 281).

---

[14]Hartman's discussion of "resistance" (in *To the Lighthouse*) helps clarify the struggle involved here. *Beyond Formalism*, p. 73.

Heidegger's lecture defines dread as man's anxiety over having nothing to rely on save his own courage to be. In discussing the effects of dread he utilizes a linguistic example that illuminates the passage above as well as Virginia Woolf's persistent use of the indefinite pronoun "one": "In dread we are 'in suspense' (*wir schweben*). Or, to put it more precisely, dread holds us in suspense because it makes what-is-in-totality slip away from us. Hence we too, as existents in the midst of what-is, slip away from ourselves along with it. For this reason it is not 'you' or 'I' that has the uncanny feeling, but 'one.' In the trepidation of this suspense where there is nothing to hold on to, pure *Da-sein* is all that remains."[15]

The sense of Septimus' suicide as somehow "her disaster—her disgrace" leads the heroine to confess that she has led an inauthentic life: "She had wanted success. Lady Bexborough and the rest of it." But through her self-deprecation at having "lost herself in the process of living" come recollections of moments when the shield has glimmered and she has perceived, like Wordsworth, a depth in experience. Walking to the window she is shocked to see the old lady a second time, now staring straight at her under a sky whose solemnity is more than romantic orchestration: "She was going to bed. And the sky. It will be a solemn sky, she had thought, it will be a dusky sky, turning away its cheek in beauty. But there it was—ashen pale, raced over quickly by tapering vast clouds. It was new to her. The wind must have risen. She was going to bed, in the room opposite. It was fascinating to watch her, moving about, that old lady, crossing the room, coming to the window. Could she see her?" (p. 283).

The gulf that separates one room from the other is now a mysterious and enveloping presence through which the old lady (who initially gained Clarissa's consciousness as an alternative to Miss Kilman) appears miraculously free of all intentions; like the sky she is no object but a presence that involves Clarissa's joyous response. Septimus' death has expanded the heroine's world: "The clock began striking. The young man had killed himself; but she did not pity him; with the clock striking the hour, one, two, three, she did not pity him, with all this going on. There! the old lady had put out her light! the whole house was dark now with this going on, she repeated, and the words came to her, Fear no more the heat of the sun. She must go back to them. But what an extraordinary night! She felt somehow very like him—the young man who had killed himself" (p. 283). The extraordinary strangeness of "all this" (her phrase includes the party behind her and the scene before her) evokes wonder in Clarissa that requires history, not death, to sustain it. Like the

[15]"What is Metaphysics?", p. 336.

narrator of Keats's ode, she returns to the "sole self" through whose artistry alone vision achieves historicity. Her decision to go back—"she must assemble. She must find Sally and Peter" (p. 284)—is no reversal. Resisting the temptation to withdraw, Clarissa preserves the gift of her own presence by reentering the party she has created.[16] While she remains at the close a perfect hostess, her resolve to share with her friends the life she has experienced in solitude marks her existential triumph.

As Clarissa returns to the party, Peter and Sally are criticizing their friend and hostess in terms that the novelist herself often employed against society matrons such as Mrs. Dalloway. Clarissa's world, however, held great appeal for Virginia Woolf. During the planning and composition of *Mrs. Dalloway,* her diary reveals a distaste for her heroine that camouflages a preference for upperclass decorum. The same entry refers to Joyce's *Ulysses* with snobbish condescension one might expect to hear from Lady Bruton: "the book of a self taught working man, and we all know how distressing they are, how egotistic, insistent, raw, striking, and ultimately nauseating. When one can have the cooked flesh, why have the raw?"[17]

Lytton Strachey's impression that Virginia Woolf covered Clarissa very remarkably with her own personality occasioned no disagreement from the novelist. I suspect that she was not unaware of her ambivalent feeling toward Mrs. Dalloway. It is fair to suggest that her indictment of Peter's and Sally's inability to see Clarissa is a criticism of her own prejudices. She repeatedly states that her writing was a struggle for illumination. Recording on May 26, 1924, how her efforts with *Mrs. Dalloway* have resulted in its "becoming more analytical and human . . . less lyrical," Virginia Woolf adds, as if to stress that her aim is phenomenological rather than impressionistic, that "to see human beings freely and quickly is an infinite gain to me."[18] Through *Mrs. Dalloway,* she has confronted "the other"; her creation of Clarissa Dalloway involved an existential act of self-examination.

The values of the age prevent Sally and Peter from seeing Clarissa. Sally's passion for success leads her to assume that Clarissa has left the party to cultivate more important guests. (Peter accounts for her absence on the same grounds.) While Sally's despair of relationship—"she often

---

[16]One of Sigmund Freud's late comments on the artist, quoted by Ernest Jones, seems particularly relevant: "The artist, like the neurotic, had withdrawn from an unsatisfying reality into this world of imagination; but, unlike the neurotic, he knew how to find a way back from it and once more to get a firm foothold in reality." *The Life and Work of Sigmund Freud,* vol. III (New York: Basic Books, 1957), p. 421.

[17]*Writer's Diary,* p. 46.

[18]Ibid., p. 61.

went into her garden and got from her flowers a peace which men and women never gave her" (pp. 293–294)—characterizes an important theme of the novel, she remains ironically loyal to the predilections of English society. Countering Clarissa Dalloway's social accomplishments with her own less subtle sense of success, she assures all that she has done things too: "I have five sons" (p. 284).

Both friends are quick to condemn as snobbery Clarissa's failure to reach them. They assume that to communicate she must renounce her world for theirs: a world of emotion recollected in tranquility. Sally, and to a lesser extent Peter, have chosen to live largely in retrospect, preserving autonomy against the unexpected intrusion of foreign ideas and unsettling passions. Significantly, Clarissa responds with affection to those alien qualities in Sally she might well censure: "She [Sally] had the simplest egotism, the most open desire to be thought first always, and Clarissa loved her for being still like that" (p. 261).

Sally's life is over—it is the young who are beautiful, she tells her companion as they watch the Dalloways' youthful daughter. Clarissa, rejuvenated by the presence of an old woman, authenticates the existential faith that man is the future of man; reentering the party she reconstitutes the meaning that defines her life.[19]

While Peter argues with Sally's repudiation of others, Clarissa serves to recall the image of himself he wants to remember: the martyr of objective time and an insensitive society. His supposed independence, his affirmation of privacy as a state in which "one may do as one chooses," masks his own difficulties. As Peter himself admits (echoing Clarissa's earlier observation): "it had been his undoing" (p. 230).

The confusion is part of Peter's makeup. While he replies to Sally that he prefers human beings to cabbages (a phrase that Clarissa recalls when she first thinks about her former fiancé), throughout the novel he asserts a preference for solitude. "Now, at the age of fifty-three," he tells us in Regent Park following his sexual fantasy, "one scarcely needed people any more" (p. 119). The instant of sunshine, like the make-believe escapade with the young woman he has trailed, is enough to sustain his self-centered world. Even Daisy, the woman he intends to marry, exists in his mind as a weapon against Clarissa and as a mirror for indulging his Byronic pose.

Clarissa's message—"Heavenly to see you"—that he finds waiting at his hotel," was like a nudge in the ribs. Why couldn't she let him be?"

[19]John Graham, in his fine article, "Time in the Novels of Virginia Woolf," *University of Toronto Quarterly*, 18 (January 1949), discusses Clarissa's return to the party in terms of her capacity to conquer time, pp. 189–190.

(p. 234). Although he asserts that "nothing would induce him to read it again," his romantic self-pity requires the love of a woman that cannot be his. Peter's vow never again to allow a woman to hurt him as Clarissa has is sham. He maintains at great expense the torment that defines and victimizes him. His plea for her to "let him be" is the ironic inversion of Clarissa's respect for the independence of others.

Peter and Sally, however, are no less human by virtue of their inauthenticity. The fear that drives them to dominate others is stamped upon Clarissa's world and no doubt our own. If Peter has denied (more than once) the sanctity of the human heart by reducing Clarissa to "the perfect hostess," on other occasions he has responded to such mystery. Early in the book he describes the magical quality of her parties. Clarissa, he confesses, has "that extraordinary gift, that woman's gift, of making a world of her own wherever she happened to be." During her parties it was not what she did or said that one remembered but rather the extraordinary sense of her being there, "There she was" (pp. 114–115).

In the closing scene, as Clarissa moves from her small room toward Peter, her miraculous presence fills him once again with an undefinable sense of terror and ecstasy; reduced to wonder he can only exclaim: "It is Clarissa." The novel's last words, reiterating Peter's messianic invocation —"For there she was"—challenge each critic's effort to fathom Mrs. Dalloway. Is the statement a final irony—Peter's romantic affirmation of a presence that sustains his melancholy—or does the reader respond with similar apostolic fervor to Clarissa as being there in some special way?[20] Since Virginia Woolf sought to portray the mysterious reality of character it is fitting that, finally, this question remains unanswered.

[20]Martin Heidegger's discussion of "the temporality of resoluteness" and the manner in which "a moment of vision . . . makes the situation authentically present," serves as an illuminating gloss on the closing section of the novel. *Being and Time,* trans. John Macquarrie and Edward Robinson (New York: Harper & Row, 1962), p. 463.

Julia Carlson

The Solitary Traveller in Mrs. Dalloway

The most enigmatic pages of *Mrs. Dalloway* occur in a self-contained section early in the novel where Virginia Woolf describes a solitary traveller's homeward journey from a wood to his landlady's kitchen. His experiences on this journey revolve around his encounters with three women: an imaginary woman whom he shapes from sky and branches, a woman whom he sees standing in a village, and his landlady. All of these persons including the solitary traveller move in a dreamlike world alien from that of the rest of the novel. They remain nameless and are never mentioned again.

Criticism of *Mrs. Dalloway* does not explore this section sufficiently. Dismissing it as beautiful and ambiguous,[1] critics fail to ask why Virginia Woolf incorporated the solitary traveller passage into a novel she claims to have designed so that "every scene would build up the idea of C's [Clarissa Dalloway's] character."[2] Most of those critics who discuss the episode rightly indicate that it is in some way linked with Peter Walsh's relationship with Clarissa. However, they focus on only one of its two sections—either the solitary traveller's encounter with the spectral presence or his experiences with the village woman and the landlady

---

[1]See, for example, James Naremore, *The World Without a Self: Virginia Woolf and the Novel* (New Haven, 1973), p. 99.

[2]Berg Collection, New York Public Library, holograph notebook dated variously from November 9, 1922 to August 2, 1923. The entry here was recorded on June 18, 1923. The quotation is given in Charles G. Hoffmann, "From Short Story to Novel: The Manuscript Revisions of Virginia Woolf's *Mrs. Dalloway,*" *Modern Fiction Studies,* 14 (Summer, 1968), p. 183.

—and fail to interpret the passage fully or conclude, as does Reuben Brower, that it ultimately has little relevance to the rest of the novel.[3]

The positioning of the passage naturally links it with the experience of Peter Walsh, Clarissa's first suitor, who returns to London from India on the morning of the day of the novel after an absence of many years. Following his arrival, Peter visits Clarissa at the Dalloways' Westminster home, aimlessly follows a young woman on the London streets, and then, after seating himself beside a nurse, naps in Regent's Park. Here, immediately after Peter falls asleep, Virginia Woolf places the solitary traveller passage.

Although the passage occurs while Peter sleeps, it is not simply an interlude during which he dreams. Virginia Woolf exploits this time to provide the reader with a key to Peter's experience in the novel. His presentation as a solitary traveller is particularly apt, for the journey the solitary traveller makes mirrors Peter's lonely movement through society. Just as the solitary traveller's failure to make fulfilling human contact with the marvelous spectral presence, the village woman, and the landlady leaves him companionless, Peter's inability to maintain satisfying relationships with Clarissa, with his former wife, and with Daisy, his Indian mistress, forces him to live in emotional isolation. Throughout his life Peter has been a loner, a wanderer uncomfortable in society, incapable of wholeheartedly immersing himself in its activities. While visiting Clarissa's father's family home at Bourton during his youth, he painfully realizes his alienation from everyone else: "he had a feeling that they were all gathered together in a conspiracy against him—laughing and talking—behind his back."[4] As he grows older, Peter cannot conform to the traditional codes of society. His repeated blunders make him a misfit in Anglo-Indian circles: he becomes involved with Indian rather than English or Anglo-Indian women; he neglects to go to the Oriental Club in London, the usual gathering place of Anglo-Indians; and his utter lack of self-control prevents him from moving gracefully through society's drawing rooms: "It had been his undoing—this susceptibility—in Anglo-Indian society; not weeping at the right time, or laughing either" (p. 230). While Peter's actions in part precipitate his estrangement from his companions, he likewise protects himself from others by adopting a

[3]For a discussion of the first half of the episode see Jean O. Love, *Worlds of Consciousness: Mythopoetic Thought in the Novels of Virginia Woolf* (Berkeley, 1970), p. 155. For a discussion of the second half of the section see Francis Mollach, "Thematic and Structural Unity in *Mrs. Dalloway,*" *Thoth,* V (1964), p. 64. Reuben Brower, "Something Central Which Permeated: Virginia Woolf and 'Mrs. Dalloway' " in *The Fields of Light: An Experiment in Critical Reading* (New York, 1962), p. 135.

[4]Virginia Woolf, *Mrs. Dalloway* (New York: Harcourt, Brace, 1925), p. 93. Hereafter, all page references to this novel will be included in the text.

critical stance that prohibits him from engaging his emotions. As he moves within social circles, then, Peter remains, like the solitary traveller, essentially an aloof outsider.

The manner in which Virginia Woolf shapes the solitary traveller episode into a key to Peter's experience is determined by his role within the novel. As Charles Hoffman indicates, Peter's most obvious function is to disclose Clarissa's past.[5] He becomes the primary tool Virginia Woolf employs in her "tunneling process," the means utilized to "dig out beautiful caves behind my characters," to "tell the past by installments, as I have need of it."[6] As he remembers his and Clarissa's past throughout the novel, Peter reveals facts about her life which the other characters never discuss, providing the reader with an external view of her history.

Peter's view of Clarissa consists not only of the revelation of facts; he also appraises and strives to understand her. He is, as Clarissa establishes early in the novel, the chief critic of her character: "It was the state of the world that interested him, Wagner, Pope's poetry, people's characters eternally, and the defects of her own soul" (p. 9). Just as he arms himself and habitually pares his nails with his penknife, Peter criticizes Clarissa, slicing through her cool exterior to tap the vulnerable quick of her character. While she has been the object of both his admiration and contempt since their youth, it is only after their reunion abruptly thrusts their past into his middle-aged present that Peter becomes acutely conscious of his inability to explain Clarissa's behavior. As the novel unfolds, Peter, obsessed by his need to understand her, conducts the reader on a search for a comprehensive definition of her character which complements her subjective quest for identity.

Here the solitary traveller episode becomes of critical importance, for its primary function is to provide insight into Peter's struggle to define Clarissa. The passage provides a symbolic account of Peter's experience, a microcosmic view of his conception both of her and his relationship with her.

The structures of the solitary traveller's experiences and Peter's experiences with Clarissa are strikingly parallel: both undergo three journeys that terminate in meetings with women. The first woman whom the solitary traveller encounters, the spectral presence, awaits him at the end of his ride in the wood. Later, his fantasy that a village woman whom he sees standing in her doorway looks for his return marks his reentry into the ordinary world, and last, he is met by his landlady upon going back to his rooms. Similarly, Peter meets Clarissa at the end of each of his journeys in London. The first of these, his voyage from India to London,

[5]Hoffmann, op. cit., pp. 175, 182.
[6]Virginia Woolf, *A Writer's Diary,* Leonard Woolf (ed.) (London: 1969), pp. 60–61.

closes when he appears, immediately following his arrival, at the Dalloways' home. It is also Clarissa who compels him to terminate his adventure with the young woman on the London streets: "Clarissa's voice saying, Remember my party, Remember my party, sang in his ears. . . . It was over" (p. 81). Finally, his comprehensive vision of Clarissa—"For there she was"—concludes the novel, his and Clarissa's day's journey (p. 296).

Implicit in the solitary traveller passage is the indication that the solitary traveller knows only women who inhabit contrasting spheres: one of ecstasy and one of terror. The spectral presence who elates him exists in a purely visionary world; the real village woman and the landlady move in a world in which he finds only pain. After his meetings with these women, the solitary traveller's concluding question—"But to whom does the solitary traveller make reply?"—reveals that he has been utterly bewildered by his experiences with women and that he does not know whether to believe in his visionary or mortal women. He only knows that he cannot conceive of a world in which they are united, a world where he can reply to them both.

By presenting these two types of women, the solitary traveller episode prefigures Peter's analysis of Clarissa, beginning after he awakens in Regent's Park. Here it becomes clear that the women whom the solitary traveller encounters are, in effect, Clarissa. Just as the solitary traveller is perplexed by his experiences with women, Clarissa baffles Peter and he cannot determine which of the Clarissas he encounters is the "real" Clarissa.

As Peter attempts to define Clarissa, remembering his dream of Bourton and then recollecting the Clarissa of his youth, he shapes the dichotomy he perceives within her into a fact of her life, of *Mrs. Dalloway*. He indicates that the split in her personality first surfaced for him at Bourton:

> It was at Bourton that summer, early in the 'nineties, when he was so passionately in love with Clarissa. . . . They were talking about a man who had married his housemaid, one of the neighbouring squires, he had forgotten his name. He had married his housemaid, and she had been brought to Bourton to call—an awful visit it had been. She was absurdly over-dressed, "like a cockatoo," Clarissa had said, imitating her, and she never stopped talking. On and on she went, on and on. Clarissa imitated her. Then somebody said—Sally Seton it was—did it make any real difference to one's feelings to know that before they'd married she had had a baby? . . . He could see Clarissa now, turning bright pink; somehow contracting; and saying, "Oh, I shall never be able to speak to her again!" Whereupon the whole party sitting round the tea-table seemed to wobble. It was very uncomfortable.

> He hadn't blamed her for minding the fact, since in those days a girl brought up as she was, knew nothing, but it was her manner that annoyed him; timid; hard; something arrogant; unimaginative; prudish. "The death of the soul." He had said that instinctively, ticketing the moment as he used to do—the death of her soul (pp. 88–89).

Her unqualified dismissal of the housemaid signals to Peter that Clarissa has withdrawn from life and cannot accommodate the unexpected within her world, that she is fragmented. She becomes for him, at this youthful point in her life, two women: the cold Clarissa who cannot give of herself and the Clarissa who can empathize.

As he further examines his relationship with Clarissa, Peter reveals that, since the incident at Bourton, she has never reconciled the elements of her dual personality. Instead, she has continued to inhabit two worlds, to be at times compassionate, like the solitary traveller's spectral presence, and at other times, like the village woman and the landlady, a woman whose indifference torments him. Peter cannot admire the latter Clarissa, the Clarissa who banished the housemaid and whom he labels "the perfect hostess" (p. 93); she is shallow—"at her worst—effusive, insincere" (p. 254); her goals are trivial: "The obvious thing to say of her was that she was worldly; cared too much for rank and society and getting on in the world" (p. 115). She prevents him from ever knowing her: "That was the devilish part of her—this coldness, this woodenness, something very profound in her, which he had felt again this morning talking to her, an impenetrability" (p. 91). Just as the solitary traveller's landlady does not encourage him to embrace her and he is denied contact with the village woman by her refusal to acknowledge his return home, this Clarissa's tinselly charm and formidable aloofness thwart Peter's every attempt to create with her a fulfilling relationship.

Equally present in his encounters with Clarissa is the other Clarissa, a sympathetic woman with whom Peter can weep, laugh, and talk endlessly. She replicates the solitary traveller's spectral presence. They are linked with the same images: roses, the sea, the color green. The visions "are dashed in his [the solitary traveller's] face like bunches of roses" (p. 86); Clarissa surrounds herself with roses—they are "the only flowers she could bear to see cut" (p. 182). Clarissa appears before Peter at her party in a "silver-green mermaid's dress. Lolloping on the waves . . ." (p. 264); the visions murmur in the solitary traveller's ear like sirens lolloping away on the green sea waves . . ." (p. 86). This Clarissa has compassion for Peter; he can confide in her, tell her everything, "for in some ways no one understood him, felt with him as Clarissa did" (p. 68). With her he has known moments of incomparable bliss: "He had never felt so happy in the whole of his life! . . . He had twenty minutes of perfect happiness. . . . They went in and out of each other's minds without any effort'' (p. 94). However, just as the spectral presence vanishes and prevents the solitary traveller from consummating his relationship with her, Peter can never sustain a relationship with this Clarissa, for the cold Clarissa always intervenes and aborts the burgeoning harmony he and the empathic Clarissa have established.

To underline the nature of Clarissa's complexity, Virginia Woolf silhouettes the simplicity of Peter's attachments with other women against the intricacy of his and Clarissa's relationship. Seen only briefly through Peter's eyes, these women, those he is involved with in India and the unidentified young woman he follows in London, become exaggerated types who exist wholly in one or the other of the two worlds between which Clarissa continually vacillates. Peter shapes the young woman into his vision of the ideal woman, a woman who is, in effect, a superhuman form of the warm Clarissa. The illusory comfort this woman promises Peter momentarily enables him to envision an escape from his real life into a utopia: she calls to him "through hollowed hands his name, not Peter, but his private name which he called himself in his own thoughts" (p. 79); her cloak blows out to him "with an enveloping kindness, a mournful tenderness, as of arms that would open and take the tired" (p. 79). Conversely, the Indian women with whom Peter actually has relationships embody aspects of the colder Clarissa. They are superficial, silly, and no longer attract him; he has come to find them despicable, remembering his wife as "a perfect goose" and Daisy as a burden whom he no longer wishes to marry (p. 289). Through the contrast she establishes between these three relationships and Peter's with Clarissa, Virginia Woolf indicates that while he can cope with the separate elements of Clarissa's personality, he cannot withstand its full impact: whereas he can dismiss his adventure with the young woman as "an exquisite amusement" and admits that his disillusionment with both Daisy and his former wife is complete, Peter's contempt for Clarissa is continually bated by his hope that he will be able to recover the rapture her compassion has brought him (p. 81).

As Peter discovers and defines the dichotomy within Clarissa, she simultaneously reveals its existence during her self-examination. Early in the novel she indicates that her fear of the irrational, "the heat o' the sun/ . . . the furious winter's rages," passion and death, often forces her to encase herself in her social identity (p. 13). When she does, she moves in a protective world of appearances, a world where she never has to reveal herself. Society defines her and provides her with a secure facade: she is Mrs. Richard Dalloway, wife, mother, hostess.

Throughout the novel, Clarissa can never completely escape into her social role; she is always tormented by her awareness of the underside of her life. Her frigidity in her relationship with Richard haunts her. As a mother, she dreads the influence of her daughter's tutor, the domineering Doris Kilman, yet is afraid to dismiss her because of the turbulent scenes that could follow. Although she knows she must come to terms with her fears, Clarissa continues to avoid facing them until she is forced to at her party.

At this party the two spheres of inner terror and contrived harmony between which Clarissa has vacillated since the incident at Bourton clash for the second time in *Mrs. Dalloway*. Here, the comment by one of her guests, Lady Bradshaw, the wife of a psychiatrist, about the suicide of one of her husband's patients earlier that evening shatters the order of Clarissa's party and her seemingly inviolable world: "Oh! thought Clarissa, in the middle of my party, here's death, she thought" (p. 279). Embodying the irrationality from which she has striven to escape, the death, like the housemaid's pregnancy at Bourton, challenges her to confront its blatant, anarchic reality. She does confront it by leaving her party and retreating alone into an empty room. As her imagination details the suicide, her social identity vanishes. She accepts the fact of death as an "embrace" and identifies with the young man, thereby reconciling herself to the side of life which had previously terrified her:

> A thing there was that mattered; a thing, wreathed about with chatter, defaced, obscured in her own life, let drop every day in corruption, lies, chatter. This he had preserved. Death was defiance. Death was an attempt to communicate; people feeling the impossibility of reaching the centre which, mystically, evaded them; closeness drew apart; rapture faded, one was alone. There was an embrace in death. . . . the words came to her, Fear no more the heat of the sun. . . . She felt somehow very like him—the young man who had killed himself (pp.280–281, 283).

Although Clarissa unifies herself and achieves equanimity by re-creating and accepting the suicide, her reintegration is not complete for the reader until Peter Walsh recognizes her wholeness on her return to her party. In the closing words of the novel he reveals that he now knows to whom he, as the solitary traveller, must reply, that his and the reader's quest for a definition of Clarissa's character has ended. Peter's final thoughts at once provide a comprehensive definition of her and the answer he has so earnestly sought. No longer divided against herself, Clarissa holds in tension Peter's two Clarissas:

> What is this terror? what is this ecstasy? he thought to himself. What is it that fills me with extraordinary excitement?
>
> It is Clarissa, he said.
>
> For there she was (p. 296).

Ruby Cohn

Art in To the Lighthouse

When Mr. Ramsay lands on the lighthouse rock, Lily Briscoe finishes her painting. All critics agree on the intimate and essential relation between these final events of Virginia Woolf's *To the Lighthouse*. [1] Several critics have commented, too, on how Lily Briscoe's painting structures the book. [2] But there has not been adequate appreciation of the way in which the theme of art functions in *To the Lighthouse*. Neither Leonard Woolf's term "psychological poem" nor Virginia Woolf's own hesitant suggestion of "elegy" succeeds in classifying the book, for, in part at least, it is a work of art about art—as are *Hamlet* and

[1] Quotations from *To the Lighthouse* are from the Harbrace Modern Classics edition (New York: Harcourt, Brace, 1927).

[2] For example:

Bernard Blackstone, *Virginia Woolf* (London, 1949), pp. 99–130.

David Daiches, *Virginia Woolf* (Norfolk, 1942), pp. 79–96.

S. H. Derbyshire, "An Analysis of Mrs. Woolf's *To the Lighthouse*," *College English, III* (January, 1942), 353–360.

Norman Friedman, "The Waters of Annihilation: Double Vision in *To the Lighthouse*," *ELH XII* (March, 1955), 61–79.

James Hafley, *The Glass Roof* (Berkeley, 1954), pp. 77–92.

Dorothy Hoare, *Some Studies in the Modern Novel* (London, 1938), pp. 53–62.

Charles Hoffman, *"To the Lighthouse,"* *Explicator* X (November, 1951), 13.

Jean-Jacques Mayoux, *Vivants Piliers* (Paris, 1960) pp. 201–228.

Glenn Pedersen, "Vision in *To the Lighthouse*," *PMLA*, LXXXIII (December, 1958), 585–600.

John Hawley Roberts, " 'Vision and Design' in Virginia Woolf," *PMLA*, LXI (September, 1946), 842–847.

Ruby Cohn, "Art in To the Lighthouse," Modern Fiction Studies, *vol. 8, no. 2, Summer, 1962, pp. 127–136. Modern Fiction Studies,* © *1962, by Purdue Research Foundation, West Lafayette, Indiana.*

Don Quixote; as is much of the creation of artists so various as Yeats, Braque, Pirandello, Mann.

To the Lighthouse, serving to exorcise her parents' dominance,[3] absorbing her by the opportunities it provided for perfecting her "method," astonished its author by the spontaneous fluidity of its composition. In her diary Virginia Woolf comments on the "quick and flourishing attack on *To the Lighthouse*," on her "dashing fluency," on writing "as fast and freely as I have written in the whole of my life."

The first notes on the novel appear May 14, 1925:

> This is going to be fairly short; to have father's character done complete in it; and mother's; and St. Ives; and childhood; and all the usual things I try to put in—life, death, etc. But the centre is father's character, sitting in a boat, reciting We perished, each alone, while he crushes a dying mackerel.

On July 20, 1925, when she had meditated on the novel for at least two months, but had not yet begun writing, Virginia Woolf summarized it: "Father and mother and child in the garden; the death; the sail to the Lighthouse . . . (I conceive the book in 3 parts: 1. at the drawing room window; 2. seven years passed; 3. the voyage.)"

There is no published record of when or why she modified the plot, if not the basic design, to include Lily Briscoe and her art; perhaps the very rapidity and verve of composition precluded an awareness of the new theme in the novel. Only when *To the Lighthouse* was nearly completed does the diary make its first mention of Lily. On September 3, 1926, Virginia Woolf noted:

> The novel is now easily within sight of the end, but this, mysteriously, comes no nearer. [It was actually completed January, 1927.] I am doing Lily on the lawn; but whether it's her last lap, I don't know. . . . The problem is how to bring Lily and Mr. R. together and make a combination of interest at the end. . . . I had meant to end with R. climbing on to the rock. If so, what becomes of Lily and her picture? Should there be a final page about her and Carmichael looking at the picture and summing up R.'s character? In that case I lose the intensity of the moment. If this intervenes between R. and the lighthouse, there's too much chop and change, I think. Could I do it in a parenthesis? So that one had the sense of reading the two things at the same time?

Ending on Lily and her vision rather than Mr. Ramsay on the rock, Virginia Woolf nevertheless did—it is generally agreed—achieve the

[3]See Virginia Woolf's journal entries published in *A Writer's Diary* (New York, 1954). Also, Frank Baldanza, "*To the Lighthouse* Again," *PMLA*, LXX (June, 1955), 548–552.

desired effect of simultaneity. Critical disagreement begins with the interpretation of that simultaneity.

During the time she wrote *To the Lighthouse*, Virginia Woolf made the usual miscellaneous entries in her diary—reactions to reception of *The Common Reader* and *Mrs. Dalloway* (both published in 1925); remarks on landscapes, books, moods, and friends; descriptions of meeting George Moore, of visiting Thomas Hardy; some sketchy reflections on life and art. Nothing notably different from the diary entries of other years; nothing that yields a clue as to why the theme of art should have been woven into the very fabric of her fiction, instead of remaining confined to journal, lecture, and essay, as in former years. But art is central to this novel; in Part I there are ubiquitous if disparate references, and in Part III art emerges as a major motif.

If, as our first approximation, life and art are viewed as polar opposites in *To the Lighthouse*, Mrs. Ramsay and Lily Briscoe may be regarded as their respective exponents. The former opens the novel, and the latter closes it, as the stuff of life may be converted, through a particular medium, to a work of art. And indeed, in our first view of her, Mrs. Ramsay is already the subject of Lily's painting. As personification or as abstraction, life is larger than art; thus, Mrs. Ramsay, and not Lily Briscoe, is the main character of the novel; Mrs. Ramsay's tendency to exaggerate is in marked contrast to Lily's diffidence; Part I, in which Life dominates, is almost twice the length of Part III, in which Art is the focal center.

Whereas art needs life to nourish it, life is often unaware of the power of art to give it permanence. Thus, although Lily the painter is in love with Mrs. Ramsay (and, by extension, with all her family and their diverse doings), the latter cannot take Lily's painting seriously. Thus, too, Mrs. Ramsay's quite literal short-sightedness is played against Lily's "vision." Lily finds it ironic that "Mrs. Ramsay presid[ed] with immutable calm over destinies which she completely failed to understand." More subtly, Virginia Woolf suggests that life may be its own worst enemy, even as the artist may rebel against art's strict exigencies. Although it is only momentary, Mrs. Ramsay "felt alone in the presence of her old antagonist life." In Part III, staring at her canvas, Lily is "drawn out of gossip, out of living, out of community with people into the presence of this formidable ancient enemy of hers . . . this form . . . roused one to perpetual combat."

Even as a first approximation, however, the two women are not monolithic symbols, but reveal vivid personalities behind their major meaning.[4] It is not "artistic" Lily but "living" Mrs. Ramsay who is

[4]My interpretation does not preclude others, and I particularly admire those of Friedman and Mayoux.

endowed with rare beauty, for all her incongruous deer-stalker's hat and galoshes. Both women have a slightly exotic quality—Lily her Chinese eyes, and Mrs. Ramsay a Hellenic face. Both women dress soberly in grey. In spite of her easy, direct spontaneity; we never become familiar enough with Mrs. Ramsay to learn her first name, but Mrs. Ramsay calls Lily by her Christian name, suggesting the pure virgin which, by Part III, when she is forty-four (Virginia Woolf's own age when she wrote the novel), becomes "a skimpy old maid, holding a paintbrush." These humanizing details root the character to a literal ground, so that they never become figures of allegory, but rather magnetic poles for particular lines of force.

In Part I, Mrs. Ramsay is at the heart of all the busy, indiscriminate activities of her large family and her too numerous summer guests. "Her masterfulness, her positiveness, something matter-of-fact in her" lead her to manage other people's lives, from trivial to important aspects. Lily, in contrast, can barely manage to manipulate her paint-brushes, and shrinks from any strange eye on her canvas. By Part III, Lily has become aware of a fundamental difference between herself and Mrs. Ramsay. The latter, though falling occasionally into meditation, "disliked anything that reminded her that she had been seen sitting thinking." But "Some notion was in both of them [Lily the painter and Mr. Carmichael the poet] about the ineffectiveness of action, the supremacy of thought."

Mrs Ramsay, to be sure, bends all efforts to render her actions effective: first and foremost, she supplies emotional sustenance for her husband and children (when she dies, they are left in the chaotic confusion of the opening of Part III); she is an irrepressible matchmaker; she feels protective towards the whole male sex; she helps the poor and the sick; she strives for the unity and integrity of social scenes such as her dinner party. Quite explicitly, Lily Briscoe acknowledges Mrs. Ramsay's manipulation of life: "Mrs Ramsay saying, 'Life stand still here'; Mrs. Ramsay making of the moment something permanent (as in another sphere Lily herself tried to make of the moment something permanent)." Ironically, Mrs. Ramsay is seen "making" while Lily merely "tried." But Mrs. Ramsay's efforts are doomed from the start; life can *not* stand still; time *must* pass; only "in another sphere" can moments be given permanence. Mrs. Ramsay has the rare faculty of ordering a scene so that it is "like a work of art," but Lily Briscoe creates the concrete work of art.

From our first view of Lily, "standing on the edge of the lawn painting," to the significant final view, "Yes, she thought, laying down her brush in extreme fatigue, I have had my vision"—the insistence is upon her art. Although fearful lest anyone look at her canvas, she paints with stubborn integrity to her vision, in the bright colors which Mr. Paunceforte's pastels have rendered unfashionable. It is the resolution to move her tree to the center of the canvas that sustains her through the dinner party, protects her against Charles Tansley's pronouncement that women cannot paint or write, and enables her to resist Mrs. Ramsay's determination to marry her to William Bankes. By Part III, Lily's paint-brush has become for her "the one dependable thing in a world of strife, ruin, chaos." She seems more sure of her technique: the lines are nervous, but her brush-strokes are decisive. It is she who imagines the artistic credo of Mr. Carmichael: "how 'you' and 'I' and 'she' pass and vanish; nothing stays; all changes; but not words, not paint." Yet even then, even to the final brush-stroke that brings the novel to a close, she continues to be haunted by the problematical and shifting relationship of art and life.

Lacking the self-sufficient absorption of Mr. Bankes in his science, of Mr. Carmichael in his poetry, Lily is constantly attracted or repelled by—never indifferent to—the life that surrounds her, and her art is intimately related to that life. Unlike the tourist painters who set their easels facing the bay, so as to paint the evanescent lighthouse, Lily turns her gaze on house and hedge, mother and child; she absorbs all the unpredictable storm and calm of Ramsay life; she is in love with the Ramsays precisely because they abound in life, as does the sea that surrounds their island:

> The sky stuck to them; the birds sang through them. And, what was even more exciting . . . how life, from being made up of little separate incidents which one lived one by one, becomes curled and whole like a wave which bore one up with it and threw one down with it, there, with a dash on the beach.

The very redundancy of "ones" emphasizes the basic unity of life through all its diverse manifestations. Thus, in her painting of Part I, Lily converts Mrs. Ramsay and James to a single purple triangle. During the dinner party, Lily comes to see that the tree (with which Mrs. Ramsay has earlier identified herself) must be placed at the center of the canvas. By Part III, Mrs. Ramsay herself does not figure in Lily's second painting, and yet that painting is even more directly dependent upon Mrs. Ramsay's life, and upon that larger, more profound and tragic vision of life, that includes death. When Lily surprises herself by uttering Mrs. Ramsay's name aloud, it is a desperate cry that climaxes her violent need to know why life is so short and inexplicable. In this need, Lily views Augustus Carmichael, the poet, as her partner. Together they probe for the meaning of life, and convert its paint to form, beauty, and permanence: "if they shouted loud enough Mrs. Ramsay would return." Poet and painter are joined in defiance of death, in defense of life through art.

It is significant that Mr. Carmichael, poet of death, should share in Lily's vision of Mrs. Ramsay's resurrection. In Part I, he is the only character who is unresponsive to Mrs. Ramsay's beauty, who seems at times to dislike her. His opium-induced trances rebuke Mrs. Ramsay's incessant activities; the dryness of his poetic imagery is opposed to Mrs. Ramsay's immersion in sea-rhythms (and the sea is, of course, an age-old metaphor for life); his dealings with death (his poetry becomes popular only during the war) outlast Mrs. Ramsay's lifeforce. At the last, however, life and death are joined as a larger life; the painter of life and the poet of death are at once and together aware of life's final achievement, the landing at the lighthouse.

Although Mr. and particularly Mrs. Ramsay may be viewed as life-symbols, their life is opposed to art only in certain aspects. At the literal level both Mr. and Mrs. Ramsay are sensitive to art, and they are variously involved with the art of literature. In Mrs. Ramsay's busy day, art is reduced to craft: knitting, cutting out pictures from magazines, tossing a shawl over a Michaelangelo, reading aloud Grimm's "Fisherman's Wife," and leafing through a poetry anthology are all in the day's doings. As for full-length books, "she never had time to read them." Indiscriminately, Mrs. Ramsay envisions her son James as a judge, a statesman, an artist. While she reads Grimm's fairy tale to her son—oblivious to its sea of life that parallels the sea of life surrounding her—she is able to watch her husband and daughter outside, to meditate on her match of Minta Doyle and Paul Rayley, to daydream about her children, defying for them the life she cannot quite define.

At night, when the dinner party is over and the children are in bed, Mrs. Ramsay joins her husband as he sits reading Scott's *Antiquary*. She repeats the verses recited at dinner, lulls herself by reading from William Browne's "Siren's Song," scarcely aware of a meaning beyond the music. She bends the final couplet of Shakespeare's Sonnet 98 to her own life, suddenly finding insubstantial the full, active hours that separate husband and wife from morning to night:

> Yet seem'd it winter still, and, you away,
> As with your shadow I with these did play.

But in our intermittent glimpses of Mr. Ramsay during the day, he storms about like a battalion rather than a shadow, and, appropriately,

Tennyson's "Charge of the Light Brigade" is the poem he quotes, indulging his penchant for reciting poetry without preamble or provocation.[5] Suiting gesture to bombast, he lays special stress on "Some one had blundered." First uttered when Jasper Ramsay shoots at the helpless birds, the line refers more specifically to Mr. Ramsay's blundering insistence that it will not be fine enough for James to make the trip to the lighthouse; more generally, Mr. Ramsay blunders by his egotistical demands upon his family, without in turn expressing his love for them. But close upon the end of the book, Mr. Ramsay is able to rectify his blunder; spontaneously, he praises his son with a "Well done" when James steers the sailboat skillfully into the lighthouse harbor. Father and son arrive together at the lighthouse.

In another significant instance, Mr. Ramsay's literary reference in Part I becomes part of the texture of his life in Part III. During Mrs. Ramsay's dinner party, Charles Tansley insists that no one reads Scott any more. After dinner, in solitary protest, Mr. Ramsay dips into the *Antiquary* (Scott's own favorite among his novels). Disdaining the major plot, Mr. Ramsay chooses the chapter which describes the sorrow in the fisherman's hut when Steenie, the fisherman, is drowned. In Part III of *To the Lighthouse*, the voyage to the lighthouse is made under the guidance of a fisherman who points out the treacherous places where other fishermen were drowned. Mr. Ramsay is equally able to respond to the humble scenes in Scott's novel, and to the real fishermen who guide him to the lighthouse. Professor though he is, his intellectuality relates to reality. Less intuitive than his wife, he nevertheless complements her in a vital rapport with, in a virtual representation of, life.

Mr. Ramsay considers his wife unlearned, but she is capable of some literary reference, and shrewdly guesses that the self-made Charles Tansley "would have liked . . . to say how he had gone not to the circus but to Ibsen with the Ramsays." When her "booby" Paul Rayley remembers the name of Vronsky "because he always thought it such a good name for a villain," she is instantly able to recognize it as coming from *Anna Karenina*. (The irony of Paul's "villain" emerges in Part III, when Paul himself, like Vronsky, takes a mistress.).

Other minor characters also display their literary culture: Mr. Bankes, the scientist, shares Mr. Ramsay's taste for Scott, and thinks it a shame that the young no longer read Carlyle. Mr. Carmichael, a poet himself, has such catholic taste in poetry that he lies awake nights reading Virgil, and is also able to complete Mr. Ramsay's quotation from "Luriana Lurilee."[6]

[5]Hafley also discusses the significance of the Tennyson poem.
[6]I have been unable to identify these verses.

Insistent as these literary strands are, they do no more in Part I than establish art as one aspect of Ramsay life. In Part III, however, when death has attacked the Ramsays, and art itself becomes a major theme, literary reference all but disappears. The single exception is Mr. Ramsay's reiterated quotation from the last stanza of Cowper's "Castaway":

> We perished, each alone.
> But I beneath a rougher sea
> Was whelmed in deeper gulfs than he.

The very isolation of the quotation in the final section of the novel calls attention to its importance. From her earliest conception of *To the Lighthouse,* Virginia Woolf associated the first of these lines with Mr. Ramsay.[7] Just before Mr. Ramsay jumps ashore at the lighthouse, he is silent: "He might be thinking, We perish, each alone, or he might be thinking, I have reached it. I have found it."

Written in the last year of Cowper's life, the description of the drowning of the castaway is turned by the poet into a personal lamentation over his own fate. Similarly, Mr. Ramsay, after the death of his wife, pleads for Lily Briscoe's sympathy, and for that of his children, James and Cam. Although he is presumably concerned with "subject and object and the nature of reality," he is intensely subjective in attitude and demand. A solitary hero in both his own and his daughter's eyes, he is also a voluble sufferer, violently calling attention to himself. But his fate, finally, is gentler than that of the castaway (or of Cowper): because he is able to verbalize his love for his son, to utter the "Well done" of praise, he is spared from the "deeper gulfs." Even if each must perish alone, Mr. Ramsay first reaches the haven of the lighthouse.

Other than the repetitions of the "Castaway" lines, Part III of *To the Lighthouse* is barren of literary reference. Although Mr. Carmichael is by that time a celebrated poet, and Lily Briscoe indulges in speculation about the kind of poetry he writes, direct quotation from his work is carefully withheld. Even more important, although Mr. Ramsay reads throughout his trip to the lighthouse, neither title nor contents of his book is ever revealed. Three times, however, attention is called to its cover "mottled like a plover's egg." There may well be a suggestion that Mr. Ramsay's intellectualism, now that he is about to express his love for his son, becomes an embryonic form of life. All Mr. Ramsay's intellectual interests of Part I—metaphysics, reciting verse, and books in general— are converted in Part III into more vital action. No longer can art be a

---

[7]See the first quotation of this article.

mere miscellaneous Ramsay energy; now that death has attacked the Ramsays, they are more fiercely alive than ever. And it is this realization that enables Lily to complete her painting.

The crucial final sentences of the novel, in which Lily Briscoe paints one clean line to finish the picture that is blurred to her sight, establishes form and synthesis through art. But form and synthesis were not present from the start; they had to be earned by the artist, in the passage of time, through suffering and love. In Part I, Lily Briscoe stays not with the Ramsays, but at a village inn. By the end of Part II, she is invited to stay at the house. In the short middle section of the novel, the very use of a lyric mode suggests the ordering action of art, while time erodes the scenes of the life conveyed in Part I. Exterior events are tersely reported within brackets, and three out of the six bracketed passages are announcements of death. Both life and death are bracketed within the large, impersonal movements of time.

Brackets also enclose a single passage in Part III; in the sections that alternate between Lily on the shore and the Ramsays on the sea, in the heart of Lily Briscoe's vision of Mrs. Ramsay, we read: [''Macalister's boy took one of the fish and cut a square out of its side to bait his hook with. The mutilated body (it was alive still) was thrown back into the sea.][8]

Punctuation and position relate the destruction of the fish to the destruction in Part II of Prue, Andrew, and Mrs. Ramsay. Before the bracketed section, Lily dissolves into tears for Mrs. Ramsay and the life she represents. After this section, Lily, controlling her anguish, returns to her picture. It is perhaps not too fanciful to relate Lily and the fish, each suffering anguish and loss, and each being thrown back into the sea of life.

When the voyage to the lighthouse is over, Mr. Carmichael, poet, holding his French novel like a trident (the sceptre of a *sea*-god), establishes communion with Lily Briscoe, artist, by announcing, ''They will have landed.'' About the voyage, Lily says, ''He has landed. . . . It is finished.'' About her picture, ''It was done; it was finished. Yes, she thought, laying down her brush in extreme fatigue, I have had my vision.''

During the course of the novel, there are several uses of the word ''vision.''[9] Very early in Part I, Lily seeks to translate ''some miserable

[8]Originally, it was Mr. Ramsay who ''crushes a dying mackerel,'' but probably in more careful preparation for his praise of his son, the fish is finally transferred to the fisherman's son.

[9]''Vision'' is a favorite word of Virginia Woolf; Roberts discusses this aspect in some detail.

remnant of her vision'' into her painting. Later, in her conversation with Mr. Bankes, when he attempts to understand what she is doing, she finds herself unable to express herself without a brush in her hand.

> She took up once more her old painting position with the dim eyes and the absent-minded manner, subduing all her impressions as a woman to something much more general; becoming once more under *the power of that vision* which she had seen clearly once and must now grope for among hedges and houses and mothers and children—her picture. (Italics added.)

Years later, in Part III, just before Lily sights the boat on its way to the lighthouse, there are three separate uses of the word on a single page (270). From the time she learned of Mrs. Ramsay's death, Lily has been haunted by a vision of Mrs. Ramsay moving swiftly, surrounded by flowers.[10]

The closing words of the book—Lily's ''I have had my vision''—follow her final brush-stroke, and link the painting both to her vision of Mrs. Ramsay, and to the arrival at the lighthouse of Mr. Ramsay and the children. Early in Part I, Mrs. Ramsay had identified herself with the third long stroke of the lighthouse. By the end of the book, her husband reaches the lighthouse only when he is capable of her own loving spontaneity towards their son. With the words ''Well done'' Mr. Ramsay moves from his metaphysics and literature to his wife's living relationship with the children. Art has led to life.

On the shore, Lily Briscoe, painter of life, and Augustus Carmichael, poet of death, are joined in their awareness of the landing at the lighthouse. Exhausted by her feeling of having helped Mr. Ramsay, exquisitely conscious of the empty drawing-room steps where Mrs. Ramsay sat in the earlier picture, finding that her painting is as blurred as her last view of the lighthouse, Lily Briscoe wields her brush in the line that unites them all, that translates vision to art. At the lighthouse from which Mrs. Ramsay is absent, in the painting from which Mrs. Ramsay is absent, her life nevertheless endures. Life has given birth to both art and life.

[10]Lily Briscoe's vision of Mrs. Ramsay is curiously like that of Charles Tansley, early in Part I.

Carolyn Heilbrun

The Androgynous Vision in To the Lighthouse

To the Lighthouse is Mrs. Woolf's best novel of androgyny. *The Waves,* to be sure, as Harvena Richter says, presents all the six characters as part of Bernard's androgynous whole. But as in the end Bernard's voice subsumes all the others, one can recognize in this novel a revolution in technique and a revelation of consciousness which, while it includes the androgynous vision, surpasses it. *To the Lighthouse* enables us to see that, just as Flaubert said: "I am Emma Bovary," so Virginia Woolf has, in a fashion, said: "I am Mr. Ramsay." For so she is. The Mrs. Ramsays not only cannot write novels, they do not even read them. What Mrs. Ramsay marks is the return of the earth mother who, deprived for centuries of all power, position, major influence, may now again be worshiped in a vein which, giving women all adoration, gives them no ability but that of "knowing," in some vaguely mystical way. Beautiful and loving, Mrs. Ramsay has thrust herself into the midst of our impoverished world and seduced us into worshiping her.

As a mother goddess, she has not only sought her power by the seduction of her sons and the denial of her daughters, she has turned over to the undiluted male power the ordering of the world: "Indeed, she had the whole of the other sex under her protection; for reasons she could not explain, for their chivalry and valour, for the fact that they negotiated treaties, ruled India, controlled finance; finally for an attitude towards herself which no woman could fail to feel or to find agreeable, something truthful, childlike, reverential; which an old woman could take from a young man without loss of dignity, and woe betide the girl—pray Heaven it was none of her daughters!—who did not feel the worth of it, and all that it implied, to the marrow of her bones!'' Her husband meanwhile envisions the world in the masculine order she has condoned: ''. . . if thought is like the keyboard of a piano, divided into so many notes, or like the alphabet is ranged in twenty-six letters all in order, then his splendid mind had no sort of difficulty in running over those letters one by one, firmly and accurately, until it had reached say, the letter Q. He reached Q. Very few people in the whole of England ever reach Q. Here, stopping for one moment by the stone urn which held the geraniums, he saw, but now far, far away, like children picking up shells, divinely innocent and occupied with little trifles at their feet and somehow entirely defenseless against a doom which he perceived, his wife and son, together in the window. They needed his protection; he gave it them. But after Q?''

It has often been noticed that this masculine ordering of the world is deficient, and most readers and critics suppose Woolf to be condemning her father, or Mr. Ramsay, for this ''masculine'' order, while exalting the ''feminine'' order of Mrs. Ramsay. But surely, if his division of truth into so artificial an order as the alphabet is life-denying, no less so is her moody and dreamy mistiness which, unable to distinguish objects on the sea, comparing itself to a wedge of darkness, demands the protection of men while undermining what truths they find. So that for her and her children the truth about the weather, one of the few determinable truths available, is turned into a ''masculine'' aggression. James, protected by her excessive maternalism, hates his father, hates his ''masculinity'' which, so the boy is led to feel, attacks her, his mother. It is only after her death that, with the parental blessing each child will always wish for—''Well done!''—James can recognize, not just the feminine quality of the lighthouse, its light, but also the masculine, the tower, stark, straight, bare—the vision he and his father share. Cam, who had as a child been attracted to the story Mrs. Ramsay was reading James, is sent away so that Mrs. Ramsay may continue the love affair with her son, the chief temptation of devoted mothers: the making of their sons into lovers.

No one has shown forth, more swiftly, more surely than Woolf the reward to women for subjection: ''Insinuating, too, as she did the greatness of man's intellect, even in its decay, the subjection of all wives . . . to their husband's labors, she made him feel better pleased with himself than he had done yet, and he would have liked, had they taken a cab, for example, to have paid for it.'' Thus the reward for female humility is to have one's cab paid for, the effect of it is to encourage male aggression in men like Charles Tansley, so that brotherly love will come to be expressed by him ''by denouncing something, by condemning somebody.'' It is Lily Briscoe who will know where he fails, who will burn with his words that women can't write, women can't paint, but who will remember, honorably, much to his credit. Lily, the nonmaternal artist, is the one who must come to the rescue of Mrs. Ramsay, the artist of life, when her dinner party is about to be doomed by Charles Tansley's sulking, and though for Mrs. Ramsay's sake Lily rescues the dinner party by flattering him, and playing the dependent role he expects of women, she privately moves the salt cellar to remind her of her painting and thinks with relief that she need not marry anyone.

Throughout *To the Lighthouse,* Mrs. Ramsay is presented as the mother goddess, the earth mother in all her beauty. So Molly Bloom will represent the earth mother in all her fecund promiscuity. But if Molly Bloom is scarcely ideal even as the fecund earth mother—do earth mothers practice coitus interruptus?—so Mrs. Ramsay is not ideal either. She must always assure herself of her fascination, and cannot bear either to express love or to be faced with men like Mr. Carmichael, whom she does not fascinate. Yet her beauty is such that all recognize it, adore it, protect it, love particularly her ineptitude with logical thought. Mr. Ramsay likes women to be vague, misty in thought. Certainly she is enchantingly beautiful. Charles Tansley regards her: "With stars in her eyes and veils in her hair, with cyclamen and wild violets—what nonsense was he thinking? She was fifty at least; she had eight children. Stepping through fields of flowers and taking to her breast buds that had broken and lambs that had fallen; with the wind in her hair." William Bankes telephones her about trains: "He saw her at the end of the line very clearly Greek, blue-eyed. How incongruous it seemed to be telephoning to a woman like that. The Graces assembling to have joined hands in meadows of asphodel to compose that face." As mother goddess, she is in the midst of what has come to be called the feminine mystique: "Why, she asked, pressing her chin on James's head, should they grow up so fast. Why should they go to school? She would have liked always to have had a baby. She was happiest carrying one in her arms. Then people might say she was tyrannical, domineering, masterful, if they chose; she did not mind. And, touching his hair with her lips, she thought, he will never be so happy again." (One may notice parenthetically that Woolf understood what we have seen Priestley observe in other connections: that no surrender to the "feminine" role protects a woman from being accused of seeking domination.)

Yet Mrs. Ramsay, with part of her being, longs to be more than the source of life for others. "All the Being and the doing, expansive, glittering, vocal, evaporated; and one shrunk, with a sense of solemnity, to being oneself, a wedge-shaped core of darkness, something invisible to others. . . . She praised herself in praising the light, without vanity, for she was stern, she was searching, she was beautiful like that light.'' Her destiny, after all, is inevitable. "It was odd, she thought, how if one was alone, one leant to inanimate things; trees, streams, flowers; felt they expressed one; felt they became one; felt they knew one, in a sense were one; felt an irrational tenderness thus (she looked at that long steady light) as for oneself. There rose, and she looked and looked with her needles suspended, there curled up off the floor of the mind, rose from the lake of one's being, a mist, a bride to meet her lover.''

It is just after this moment that Mr. Ramsay looks "into the hedge, into its intricacy, its darkness.'' But neither his impulse nor hers can bridge their inevitable polarization; they are entrapped, he is in his "masculine" order, she in her femaleness, her mother-goddess quality. Yet he, after her death, will be able to offer his children androgyny, will discover he did not need her devouring, speechless love to affirm his children's being. She, divine in her beauty, is fatal because though she has nourished and been adored, she has withheld the femininity which might have prevented the war, the terror of "Time Passes." Mrs. Ramsay, in the first section of the novel, has "presided with immutable calm over destinies [she has] completely failed to understand.''

In trying to counter the enormous beauty of Mrs. Ramsay, in trying to reveal the dangers inherent in that marvelous femininity, one must be careful not to seem wholly to condemn her. The genuine wonder of her beauty reveals the miracle of Woolf's art. As the mother of young children, at certain moments, Mrs. Ramsay is perfection; but it is the spontaneous perfection of a moment, not the accumulated understanding of a lifetime. Her knowledge is all instinctive. When James will not have the boar's head removed, and Cam cannot sleep with its bony reminder of death, Mrs. Ramsay succeeds in fudging reality: she covers the head; it is still there, she can tell James. But now it is a beautiful sight, a nest, she tells Cam, reminding the little girl of stars falling and parrots and antelopes and gardens and everything lovely. Mrs. Ramsay, leaving the room when the children are finally asleep, feels a chill and reaches to draw her shawl about her. She has used it to cover the boar's head, given the children her own protection. This is not the sort of act of which it is possible to make a lifetime's occupation.

"Time Passes," the middle and shortest section of *To the Lighthouse*, presents the hell man has made of his world; not alone hell in general, but a particular hell, the hell of World War I. As the section opens, five characters appear, all unmarried, two of them to die young. Andrew and Prue, the doomed Ramsay children, announce that it is almost too dark to see, that one can hardly tell the sea from the land. (When Mrs. Ramsay agreed to marry Mr. Ramsay, she stepped from a boat onto the land, guided by his outstretched hand.) Lily questions about a burning light, and they put it out; Mr. Carmichael, the poet, alone leaves his candle burning, since he is reading Virgil. He, the poet, is the only one in "Time Passes," the terrible period of the war, who will do something life-enhancing: he will publish a book of poems. That Mr. Carmichael should be reading Virgil is significant: Dante chose Virgil for his guide in hell.

In the hell which follows, death is both from childbirth and war; mercy is apparent only insofar as it bestows swift death. Prue, "given" in marriage on her father's arm, is sacrificed in her female role; Andrew, taken in war, is sacrificed to his male role. And Mrs. Ramsay, in a sentence of significant syntax, turns out to have died, leaving Mr. Ramsay with his arms empty: "Mr. Ramsay, stumbling along a passage one dark morning, stretched his arms out, but Mrs. Ramsay having died rather suddenly the night before, his arms, though stretched out, remained empty." Mr. Ramsay, the subject of this sentence, stretches out his arms which remain empty, the same action which followed his desire to be told she loved him, the same distress which followed his seeing the stern look on her face when he looked into the intricacy of the hedge. Mrs. Ramsay exists only in a subordinate clause, the object of his needs. At the end of the section Lily returns; the artist awakens. It is she who asks the first question in the last section, "The Lighthouse," and it is she who, in the final sentence, has her vision. It is she who joins the mother and child in the window—a purple patch—with the tiny boat that has reached the lighthouse; it is she who, by drawing a line in her drawing (the tree of the dinner party: the lighthouse?), completes her picture. She and Mr. Carmichael, the poet, the man whose marriage had failed and who had not needed anything from Mrs. Ramsay, together understand the significance of the occasion. "They had not needed to speak," Lily thinks. "They had been thinking the same things and he had answered her without her asking him anything. He stood there as if he were spreading his hands over all the weakness and suffering of mankind; she thought he was surveying, tolerantly and compassionately, their final destiny." Mr. Carmichael lets his hand fall slowly, crowning the occasion with a blessing, and she has had her vision which only androgynous art can bestow.

As to marriage, certainly that is not held forth in the novel as an ideal. The eight children, the bill for the greenhouse, the loss of friendship, and a man no longer able to do his best work: these are the aspects of marriage we view with sentiment and have, until recently, been expected naturally to condone. But what is the marriage? Mr. Ramsay has asked her life from Mrs. Ramsay, and has paid with his own professional life for her love and beauty. But when he asks Lily to have his soul comforted, she praises his boots and discovers (and how few readers with her) that it is enough. She had not needed to sacrifice herself. In homage, he ties her laces. He had borne down upon her, threatening her sense of self, but she had not offered him submission, and he had been revived with what she did offer, an understanding of the proper shape of shoes. So Mr. Bankes, with whom she was friends though they did not marry, had admired her shoes which gave her feet room. A moment's understanding between a man and a woman may be enough: one of them need not offer her whole life, nor demand a major part of his.

If in the first section, "The Window," the female impulse, attractive and enslaving, is presented, it is in the last section that the male impulse dominates, before the androgynous vision which ends the book. We applaud the father's blessing, the boy's identification with, his acceptance of, his father and his male body. But we see what happens when the female impulse is lacking: fishes, bait cut from their living bodies, are left to die slowly out of water; when the light from the lighthouse fails, ships are wrecked and men die clinging to a mast. Because Mr. Ramsay can rescue James from his unhealthy devotion to his mother, the androgynous visions which follow are possible. Cam, seeing the island now from the boat, thinks: "It was like that then, the island," and sees her home with a double vision. And as she experiences this, there spurts up "a fountain of joy," the same fountain associated with her mother throughout the first section; Cam, like her, cannot tell the points of a compass but, unlike her, does not wish to stop time, nor to step forever from a boat onto the land of femaleness. She affirms her father in his being. James, echoing her words, thinks: "So it was like that, the lighthouse one had seen across the bay all these years; it was a stark tower on a bare rock. It satisfied him. It confirmed some obscure feeling of his about his own character." But, James had thought earlier, "the other was also the Lighthouse. For nothing was simply one thing. The other Lighthouse was true too. It was sometimes hardly to be seen across the bay."

For, as Lily Briscoe thinks, "love has a thousand shapes. There might be lovers whose gift it was to choose out the elements of things and place them together and [give] them a wholeness not theirs in life. . . ."

Nigel Nicolson

Vita Sackville-West, Virginia Woolf and the Making of Orlando

[The following excerpts from Nigel Nicolson's *Portrait of a Marriage* outline the relationship between his mother, Vita Sackville-West, and Virginia Woolf. At least part of Virginia's attraction to Vita was caused by the Sackville family's rich history and its immense, self-sustaining country estate, Knole. Vita, Virginia knew, though the only child of Lionel Sackville-West, was barred by virtue of her sex from inheriting the property. It was with this in mind as well as a knowledge of Vita's Sapphic desires that Virginia Woolf in 1928 wrote *Orlando*, a book that is at once a novel, a biography, and a history of the Sackvilles. *Editor's note.*]

Vita first met Virginia on December 14, 1922, with Clive Bell; and four days later she invited her to dine at Ebury Street, with Clive and Desmond MacCarthy. She wrote to Harold [Harold Nicolson ("Hadji"), Vita Sackville-West's husband. *Editor's note.*]:

> I simply adore Virginia Woolf, and so would you. You would fall quite flat before her charm and personality. . . . Mrs. Woolf is so simple: she does give the impression of something big. She is utterly unaffected: there are no outward adornments—she dresses quite atrociously. At first you think she is plain, then a sort of spiritual beauty imposes itself on you, and you find a fascination in watching her. She was smarter last night, that is to say, the woollen orange stockings were replaced by yellow silk ones,

Excerpted from Portrait of a Marriage *by Nigel Nicolson. Copyright* © *1974 by Nigel Nicolson. Reprinted by permission of Atheneum Publishers, New York, and Weidenfeld (Publishers) Limited, London.*

but she still wore the pumps. She is both detached and human, silent till she wants to say something, and then says it supremely well. She is quite old [forty]. I've rarely taken such a fancy to anyone, and I think she likes me. At least, she's asked me to Richmond where she lives. Darling, I have quite lost my heart. [*December 19, 1922*] . . .

Her friendship was the most important fact in Vita's life, except Harold, just as Vita's was the most important in Virginia's, except Leonard, and perhaps her sister Vanessa. . . . Their marriages were alike in the freedom they allowed each other, in the invincibility of their love, in its intellectual, spiritual and nonphysical base, in the eagerness of all four of them to savor life, challenge convention, work hard, play dangerously with the emotions—and in their solicitude for each other. . . . There was no jealousy between the Woolfs and the Nicolsons, because they had arrived independently at the same definition of "trust." Leonard, perhaps, was a little less tolerant than Harold, fearing not that Virginia might cease to love him, but that the strain on her emotions might again unsettle her mind. Harold feared this too.

But let them speak for themselves. First, Virginia in her diary, still slightly defensive:

> Vita for three days at Long Barn . . . I like her and being with her and the splendour—she shines in the grocer's shop in Sevenoaks with a candle lit radiance, stalking on legs like beech trees, pink glowing, grape clustered, pearl hung. . . . What is the effect of all this on me? Very mixed. There is her maturity and full breastedness; her being so much in full sail on the high tides, where I am coasting down backwaters; her capacity I mean to take the floor in any company, to represent her country, to visit Chatsworth, to control silver, servants, chow dogs; her motherhood (but she is a little cold and off-hand with her boys) her being in short (what I have never been) a real woman. Then there is some voluptuousness about her; the grapes are ripe; and not reflective. No. In brain and insight she is not as highly organized as I am. But then she is aware of this and so lavishes on me the maternal protection which, for some reason, is what I have always most wished from everyone. . . . [Quentin Bell, *Virginia Woolf.* Vol. II., pp. 117–118].

Professor Bell speculates on how things may have developed from there: "There may have been—on balance I think there probably was—some caressing, some bedding together." I can add a little to that from Harold's and Vita's letters.

Vita to Harold: I fetched V. and brought her down here [Long Barn]. She is an exquisite companion, and I love her dearly. Leonard is coming on Saturday. Please don't think

    a) I shall fall in love with Virginia
    b) Virginia will " "   me
    c) Leonard "   "   "   "
    d) I shall "   "   "   Leonard

because it is not so. Only I know my silly Hadji will say to himself, *ça y est,* and so on. I am missing you dreadfully. I am missing you specially because V. was so very sweet about you, and so understanding. [*December 17, 1925*] . . .

Vita to Harold: I think she is one of the most mentally exciting people I know. She hates the wishy-washiness of Bloomsbury young men. We have made friends by leaps and bounds in these two days. I love her, but couldn't fall "in love" with her, so don't be nervous! [*December 19, 1925*] . . .

Harold to Vita: Oh my dear, I do hope that Virginia is not going to be a muddle! It is like smoking over a petrol tank. [*July 7, 1926*]

Vita to Harold: Darling, there is no muddle anywhere. I keep on telling you so. You mention Virginia: it is simply laughable. I love Virginia—as who wouldn't? But really, my sweet, one's love for Virginia is a very different thing: a mental thing; a spiritual thing, if you like, an intellectual thing, and she inspires a feeling of tenderness, which is, I suppose, owing to her funny mixture of hardness and softness—the hardness of her mind, and her terror of going mad again. She makes me feel protective. Also she loves me, which flatters and pleases me. Also—since I have embarked on telling you about Virginia—I am scared to death of arousing physical feelings in her, because of the madness. I don't know what effect it would have, you see: it is a fire with which I have no wish to play. I have too much real affection and respect for her. Also she has never lived with anyone except Leonard, which was a terrible failure, and was abandoned quite soon. So all that remains an unknown quantity; and I have got too many dogs not to let them lie when they *are* asleep. Besides *ça ne me rien dit;* and *ça lui dit trop,* where I am concerned. I don't want to get landed in an affair which might get beyond my control before I knew where I was.

    Besides, Virginia is not the sort of person one thinks of in that way. There is something incongruous and almost indecent in the idea. I *have* gone to bed with her (twice), but that's all. Now you know all about it, and I hope I haven't shocked you. My darling, you are the one and only person for me in the world; do take that in once and for all, you little dunderhead. [*August 17, 1926*] . . .

But *Orlando!* Imagine those two, seeing each other at least once a week, one writing a book about the other, swooping on Knole to squeeze from it another paragraph, on Long Barn to trap Vita into a new admission about her past (Violet, whom Virginia met once, comes into the book as Sasha, a Russian princess, "like a fox, or an olive tree"), dragging Vita to a London studio to have her photographed as a Lely, tantalizing her, hinting at the fantasy but never lifting more than a corner of it—until on the day before publication, *Orlando* arrived in a brown-paper parcel from the Hogarth Press, followed a few days later by the author with the manuscript as a present. Vita wrote to Harold: "I am in the middle of reading *Orlando,* in such a turmoil of excitement and confusion that I scarcely know where (or who) I am!" She loved it. Naturally she was flattered, but more than that, the novel identified her with Knole for ever. Virginia by her genius had provided Vita with a unique consolation for having been born a girl, for her exclusion from her inheritance, for her father's death earlier that year. The book, for her, was not simply a brilliant masque or pageant. It was a memorial mass.

Joanne Trautmann

Orlando *and Vita Sackville-West*

In *The Waves* Neville observes that as a writer Bernard exploits his friends for his stories, a comment resembling Vita's charge that Virginia Woolf saw everything in her life as potential copy. "We are all," Neville says, "phrases in Bernard's story, things he writes down in his notebook under A or under B." When Bernard's creator read V. Sackville-West's *Passenger to Teheran* in 1926, she wrote its author: "I kept saying, 'How I should like to know this woman' and then thinking, 'But I do,' and then 'no, I don't—not altogether the woman who writes this.' I didn't know the extent of your subtleties. . . . The whole book is full of nooks and corners which I enjoy exploring." A vaguely sexual image for this G.E. Moore exercise in the cognition of the beautiful qualities of one's friend. By October 1927 Virginia was writing *Orlando: a Biography* in which she proposed to do her exploring. She wrote to Vita about the project, seeking her agreement and cooperation: "I should like to untwine and twist again some very odd incongruous strands in you." She had, she reported, been reading *Knole and the Sackvilles:* "Dear me, you have a rich dusky attic of a mind. Oh yes, I want very much to see you." An article published after the appearance of Virginia Woolf's diary made it clear that V. Sackville-West, her family, and home were the inspirations for *Orlando.* In *The Listener* for 27 January 1955, Vita reprinted this and several other letters relating to the book. She claims not to have been deceived by Virginia's "sudden, urgent desire" to see her. She repeats

From Joanne Trautmann, The Jessamy Brides: The Friendship of Virginia Woolf *and V. Sackville-West,* The Pennsylvania State University Press, 1973. Reprinted by permission of the publisher.

an old charge: "I realized that it was the author's form of cupboard love—in other words, I had become 'copy.' "

This was by no means the first time that a person from her private life had become the model for a character in Virginia Woolf's work. There had been the Lytton-like character in *The Voyage Out,* and the portraits of her parents in *To the Lighthouse.* Quentin Bell says that he and his aunt used to write little sketches of their mutual friends and relatives (thus the joke in *Orlando's* Preface, acknowledging the aid of her nephew as "an old and valued collaborator in fiction"). She noted in her diary for 18 September 1927, a plan to write contemporary history by using biographical sketches of all her friends. Already in this plan Vita was "Orlando, a young nobleman."

Virginia Woolf knew well the main problems of the biographer. She wrote to Vita about her mystery as the author of *Passenger to Teheran:* "Do we then know nobody? Only our own versions of them, which as likely as not, are emanations from ourselves?" In the case of her proposed biography-fantasy of a friend, this problem could be turned to an advantage, personal and aesthetic. She had already shown in *To the Lighthouse* Lily's intense desire to penetrate Mrs. Ramsay's mysteries, and in doing so become one with the object adored. "Could loving, as people called it, make her and Mrs. Ramsay one?" The device Lily chooses to manifest her desire for coalescence is her painting of Mrs. Ramsay in her natural environment. Lily would create her friend. Friendship, she thinks is "like a work of art."

After the experience of *Orlando,* Virginia Woolf had an even more profound understanding of friendships. *The Waves,* her next book, shows Bernard and his friends reflecting images of each other. "We use our friends to measure our own stature." Yet this is a painful process because it means mixing one's idea of oneself with another's idea. It means being "recalled," "mitigated," and "adulterated" (compare Sackville-West's "Solitude"). Bernard's relationship with the magnificently physical Percival is a mirror image in a specific way, and related in precisely this way to Virginia and Vita. Bernard is speaking: "I recover what he was to me: my opposite. . . . My own infirmities oppress me. There is no longer him to oppose them." The platonic relationship of Bernard with Neville, though Neville is exclusively homosexual in inclination, is like that between Virginia and Vita in that both are literary friendships. The friendship of Bernard the fiction writer and Neville the poet works on an obvious level when they compare, for example, their versions of Shakespeare and learn from each other's insights. The friendship works on the level examined by Lily Briscoe when, because of their special talents as artists, they can create each other. To Neville, Bernard addresses this offer of aesthetic love: "Let me create you. (You have

done as much for me.)'' Eventually, of course, all Bernard's friends are
seen as emanations of himself. Indistinguishable from himself, they are
only several of a thousand incongruous, male and female strands from all
periods of time which twist together to form Bernard's multiple personality. Through those strands and their record in his own writing, Bernard,
like Virginia Woolf, searches for a perfect unity: "Some people go to
priests; others to poetry; I to my friends, I to my own heart, I to seek
among phrases and fragments something unbroken. . . .''

Orlando is a record of another of these searches, this time, more
directly Virginia's. The book has been critically analyzed from several
angles, as it requires. Among other categories, it may be seen as a parody
of biography, an essay in the exotic, a mock-heroic novel of ideas, an
imaginative literary and social history of England, and a biography of V.
Sackville-West. Readers of *Orlando* have normally discussed the book
without much more than superficial reference to the woman who inspired
it. Irma Rantavaara lists some of the obvious biographical parallels, then
adds: "These matter-of-fact biographical details are, however, the least
important elements." Frank Baldanza has traced out many of the biographical parallels through a careful reading of *Knole and the Sackvilles*,
from which Virginia Woolf took details, exaggerating them at will. Jean
Guiguet is intrigued by the relationship between Woolf and Sackville-
West and guesses that Virginia saw *Orlando* as a way of fulfilling herself
through Vita.

I prefer to see the book as the symbolic story of the friendship
between its author and the most important member of her audience, V.
Sackville-West, to whom the book is dedicated. In "Mr. Bennett and
Mrs. Brown" the author presses warmly for a coalition between writer
and audience. Here the figure of Orlando is a coalition between Virginia
and Vita.

This process begins with the genesis of the book. The first hint of the
"Defoe narrative" that will become *Orlando* occurs in the diary entry for
14 March 1927. There Virginia Woolf sketches out a fantasy called "The
Jessamy Brides": "Two women, poor, solitary at the top of a house."
The ladies dream about Constantinople and golden domes. Virginia
Woolf wants to have an extravagant fling with "satire and wildness."
Furthermore, "sapphism is to be suggested." At its genesis, then,
Orlando is the story, not of a single man, but of two romantic women,
sapphic brides without men: Virginia and Vita out on a fantastic spree.

Orlando retains the fantasy originally planned, but it is based as well
on truths about its subject and its author. Virginia Woolf admired a
similar approach in other biographies. In an article on "The New Biography," written about the same time as she was beginning *Orlando,*
she praised a certain biographer for doing what she was to do as she

took both Vita and herself as subject: "he has devised a method of writing about people and about himself as though they were at once real and imaginary." (The biographer she refers to is Harold Nicolson.)

Vita Sackville-West did not see a word of *Orlando* until she received a printed copy. When she looked into the mirror held up for her by her friend, she saw a fantasy figure of heroic proportions. But she recognized enough details to be flattered. Some of them were private, signs between the two of them, but there are others which we can point to as part of what we know about Vita's life. We can see the distance between the design founded on fact and the heroic image filled in with emanations from her romantic creator.

Orlando's name is taken from *As You Like It*. Shakespeare's hero is the romantic young aristocrat, cut off from his father's fortune, as Vita was cut off from Knole. Floris Delattre's theory is that Woolf's Orlando is an amalgamation of Shakespeare's Orlando and Rosalind. This is very likely. Sprightly, imaginative Rosalind, who controls the events of Shakespeare's play, would certainly appeal to Virginia Woolf. In *Night and Day* the heroine's mother calls her a Rosalind type. The merging of the two "Jessamy Brides," Vita and Virginia figures, into Orlando is parallel to this merging of Orlando the nobleman and Rosalind the quick-witted controlling spirit.

But Rosalind is seen before her marriage. If Shakespeare had had a talented sister, Virginia Woolf hypothesizes in *Orlando's* polemic, *A Room of One's Own,* she would not have had a chance to create anything except babies. So Woolf's talented young person of the sixteenth century must be male.

Fortuituously for Virginia Woolf, whose first literary loves were the Elizabethan prose writers, Elizabethan is the period in which the Sackville family produced the first of the men still remembered widely today. Starting with the first Sackville owner of Knole, Thomas, she builds her initial picture of Orlando from details of Thomas and Vita. Orlando's "fathers had been noble since they had been at all." They had been warriors. Their descendant now lives in a vast house decorated with heraldic leopards, Knole's most obvious decorative detail. This parallels Thomas Sackville's family history, which Vita traces in *Knole and the Sackvilles* back to a Norman nobleman who came over with William. "But what's 400 years of nobility, all the same?"—Virginia wrote in that first letter about *Orlando*. She may have tried to toss it off, but the impression remains that Virginia was highly romantic about this old family, and was impressed too, Quentin Bell believes. Thomas Sackville had, after all, written part of the first English tragedy. His descendants had also written and had patronized writers. There were Pope and Dryden manuscripts in the Knole library. Now, in Vita, Knole again had a resident poet. And her great friend was the writer Virginia Woolf, whose *Orlando* manuscript rests at Knole. The young Orlando sits in the attic, rapidly covering page after page with pompous poetry. This is as much Vita as Thomas, for as a young girl, she stole upstairs, her son relates, away from her unintellectual family and secretly wrote long historical novels, some in French and Italian, as Orlando's are. She had one early piece printed privately, as Orlando does.

Virginia caricatures other characteristics known to be Vita's—her sudden melancholy, her need for solitude, her love of nature. This exaggeration becomes part of the structure of the book. Virginia Woolf pictures Orlando alone on top of a hill from which he can see forty counties. Together the created Vita and her creator look at the vast view; first there in England, then in Constantinople, and then through several centuries, swooping down now and then to pick up the essential details of time and place.

Queen Elizabeth is introduced as Orlando's benefactress. She is useful because she was in fact a cousin of Thomas and did in fact make him her treasurer. Elizabeth is also valuable because her virginal attraction to Orlando is similar to the pose adopted by the author: the attracted but occasionally reticent and pedantic admirer. This stance provides a contrast with Orlando's own varied sexual adventures. Like the picaresque heroes he resembles, and also like several notorious Sackvilles, Orlando has an active love life. None of it sullies him; it merely promotes the image of a passionate, free-spirited young man. This was part of Virginia Woolf's original intention. She teases Vita about her amorousness in the letter of 9 October 1927, from which Vita delicately omitted a few words when she reprinted it in *The Listener*. Here, with my italics indicating the relevant phrase, is the line as it is found in Vita's script for the BBC broadcast on which the *Listener* article is based: "suppose Orlando turns out to be Vita, and it's all about you *and the lusts of your flesh* and the lure of your mind—heart you have none."

That last accusation, echoing Vita's charges against Virginia, takes form in Orlando's behavior during his first few affairs when he is, again like his picaresque forerunners, heartless. But he suffers when he meets Sasha because, modeled perhaps on Vita's great early love, Violet Trefusis, that princess is strange in several ways. She is, in the first place, a foreigner from a culture uncivilized in contrast to Elizabethan England. Their affair is conducted in French. Above all, Sasha's womanliness itself is mysterious to Orlando. That Virginia Woolf saw Sasha as a lesson in womanliness is suggested in part by her use of a photograph of her young niece, Angelica Bell, to stand for the princess as a child. In the midst of writing *Orlando,* Virginia described Angelica at a children's party as "so mature and composed; all grey and silver; such an epitome of all womanliness, such an unopened bud of sense and sensibility'' (*Diary,* 20 December 1927). Soft one minute, savage the next, Sasha reminds Orlando of his pet white fox. (Orlando has Vita's love of animals.) Virginia Woolf enjoyed this joking imagery. At one point Sasha even howls like a wolf. Purity and a hint of the fang, Vita ascribed to her friend. Orlando is intrigued and confused by his lady's strangeness. But there are hints that he will one day understand. There may be qualities of the other in each of them, for their clothing, like the casual clothes Vita wore, makes no blatant announcement that the wearer is either one sex or the other.

His first major love encounter ended, Orlando falls into a trance. In fact Orlando experiences two trances. The second one is a Sleeping Beauty swoon, after which the author awakens Orlando to a new life. But the first resembles Virginia Woolf's depressed periods when she retired to her bed for days or weeks, and outward life, as far as she was concerned, stopped. During these periods she felt that something "partly mystical" happened to her (*Diary,* 16 February 1930). Just as Orlando undergoes his first trance because he has experienced a loss too painful to face directly, Virginia Woolf's mind "refuses to go on registering impressions. It shuts itself up. It becomes chrysalis." Toward the end of the illness described in this diary entry, Vita calls on Virginia, and she begins to revive. Something in "Vita's life so full and flush" has awakened her, and she begins to compose again.

Similarly, Orlando awakens from his trance to find that his adolescent affliction has become a disease: he must write. He reaches this knowledge after considering, in the manner of Thomas Sackville's "Induction" to *Mirror for Magistrates,* that "all pomp is built upon corruption" and after reading the "marvelously contorted" style of one of Virginia Woolf's favorites, Sir Thomas Browne. Now none of his inherited pomp means anything to the young nobleman. Vita rather liked the gatherings of aristocratic society as a young woman, but retreated more and more into a simpler life in order to write. And so does Orlando repudiate his courtly life style. He hopes that he has a calling and that his simple tastes and his humble greatgrandmother show that he belongs "to the sacred race rather than to the noble." So did Vita glory in her grandmother Pepita and emphasize the simplicity of her homes, in spite of the servants and the silver. Orlando seeks the friendship of the writer Nick Greene, a relationship which Virginia Woolf delights in writing about. Though the writing fraternity may be sacred, it is also human. Nick Greene is a snob; his wife has a yearly baby. Later Alexander Pope speaks three brilliant epigrams and slips back into dullness. Orlando, expecting gods, is dismayed. Knowing Vita's awe of Virginia Woolf's genius, it is easy to guess that Virginia is teasing Vita about the early period of their acquaintance. Still, Nick Greene has a curious assortment of knowledge and a way with narrative which fascinates the entire household. Greene's satire against Orlando, foreshadowing, as Stephen Spender notes, Ray Campbell's *Georgiad,* drives Orlando into solitude again. He even burns his poetry, retaining only "The Oak Tree," another name for Sackville-West's "The Land," from which a few lines are quoted.

Greene's attack on Orlando's writing and Orlando's subsequent withdrawal to the contemplative life are a necessary step in his becoming a writer. Orlando here is Vita and Virginia and every writer. The external details are Vita's—Orlando trusts only dogs and roses—but the experiences are his creator's. Orlando's experiences with time seem a parody of Virginia Woolf's themes and techniques in other novels, particularly the "Time Passes" section of *To the Lighthouse.* Vita's ancient family adds depth to Virginia Woolf's sense that Orlando's past is there in every moment of the present. Eventually Orlando declares what Virginia did at age forty: he will write to please himself. Like Orlando reacting against Greene's attack, she reacts to an unfavorable review by stating that she has made a bargain with herself to be an unpopular writer (*Diary,* 17 and 18 February 1922). Virginia hopes to gain thereby "a sense of freedom," needing neither praise nor blame. Orlando chooses obscurity; even anonymity would be welcome.

In this new light he looks at his home as a work of art built over the centuries by anonymous noblemen. He determines to add what he can to this great impersonal art. This gives the author a chance to introduce more details about Knole, which she takes from the activities of Vita's ancestors in *Knole and the Sackvilles.* The author makes every attempt to understand her friend's love of Knole. In addition to Vita's book on her ancestral home, there was the evidence of several poems in *Orchard and Vineyard* (1921) about Vita's joy at returning to Knole. In *Orlando* there is something of Knole's personification for Vita. When Orlando returns home at the end of the novel and makes the customary walk through the house, the rooms are friends. Orlando and Knole have "known each other close on four centuries now. They had nothing to conceal." Virginia Woolf understands how Vita-Orlando feels now that Knole is beyond possessing. But in a way she consoles Vita for this loss through the recreation of Knole's past in *Orlando.* Woolf shows the way into the historical past which becomes simultaneous with Orlando's mental past, "the darkness where things shape themselves." In doing so, she satisfies her own sense of the continuity of events. Nigel Nicolson describes how Virginia Woolf would take his version of the events of the day and shape them imaginatively before handing them back to him, more permanently his. In *Orlando* she has played the same magical trick with Vita Sackville-West's version of Knole.

The middle part of Orlando's life is again based partly on the lives of the Sackvilles, some of whom served as ambassadors, and partly on Vita's own experiences. Only a short time before *Orlando* was written, Vita had been in Persia, surely the inspiration for much of the vaguely Middle Eastern details in this section of the book. But she had also been in Constantinople itself, to which Orlando goes as ambassador, when Harold Nicolson was on the diplomatic staff there during the war. Orlando is now "in the prime of life," and Virginia Woolf's description of his power over people is similar to Leonard's description of Vita in her prime. Orlando is said to have "the power to stir the fancy and rivet the eye. . . . The power is a mysterious one compounded of beauty, birth, and some rare gift, which we may call glamour and have done with it." The novel slips easily from this romance to a satiric evocation, in the manner of Sterne or Swift, of the life of an ambassador. In effect, this is a mock-heroic battle in Virginia's campaign to get Harold Nicolson to leave diplomacy. The story of Vita's grandmother comes in at this point, as does the debate between the aristocratic and gypsy strands in Vita's life style. Orlando, who has always romanticized the common, obscure people—a habit as much Virginia's as Vita's—marries Rosina Pepita, a dancer. This leads to Orlando's sojourn among the gypsies, where Virginia teases Vita about her family's being upstarts when compared to the gypsies' ancient heritage. More seriously, she shows Orlando's further education as a writer, an English writer with an English devotion to nature and an English aristocrat's reverence for tradition. The alliance with Rosina Pepita leads also to a comic version of the real life lawsuit following the death of Vita's grandfather, in which a son of his and Pepita's claimed inheritance of Knole.

But the most important event of Orlando's stay in Constantinople (the most important event, in fact, of his life) is his change from one sex to the other. This happens during one of those trance-retreats in which Orlando sees into "the dark hollow at the back of the head" and discovers, apparently, his womanliness. His body immediately makes the appropriate adjustments. Orlando's feminine traits will now dominate her life, though she retains all her masculine awareness as well.

Orlando becomes a woman at the age of thirty, approximately Vita's age when she first met Virginia. Thirty is also the age at which Virginia married. The age meant major new sexual experiences for both of them. At thirty Orlando is just beginning to operate fully, since until that time she has known only half of the complete, androgynous human nature.

Dressed at first in Turkish clothing of the sort which disguises the sex, Orlando must finally change to feminine clothing for her return to England, now in the eighteenth century. For a time the lady Orlando finds both sexes equally absurd. As the pursuer, she had thought Sasha's behavior incomprehensible. Now, as the pursued, she sneers at men because they are likely to trip over themselves if she shows a bit of leg. But soon she recognizes the advantages of being a woman with masculine experiences. As a woman, men will try to keep her in a position of poverty and ignorance; but she sees the pomposity of men playing at soldier and judge, and prefers those states that she thinks are more easily accessible to women: contemplation, solitude, love. She is capable of taking both masculine aggressive roles and feminine passive roles. She has a masculine knowledge of agriculture, riding, and drinking, yet she seeks no power over others. She is femininely tender, yet will not tie herself down to dull domestic chores. She discovers that her love for Sasha has now, if anything, deepened because they share a feminine consciousness. Sasha no longer seems an exciting, mysterious, but distant creature. To overcome the eighteenth-century limitations on women, Orlando, who is extraordinarily handsome, sometimes dresses in the clothing of a man and sallies forth to take in the night life. On one occasion, in a male disguise, she picks up a courtesan and is amazed to discover that she can see the girl's dishonest attempts to gratify her escort's masculinity. When Orlando drops her disguise, she and the girl quickly become close comrades, speaking freely as they can do with no man.

In her treatment of Orlando as an androgynous figure, Virginia Woolf is clearly glorifying those androgynous elements we have seen in Vita Sackville-West's appearance and values. Orlando even strides, as Vita was said to stride, and drives a car flamboyantly, as Vita did. Virginia Woolf investigates the emotional aspects of Vita's lesbian interests, and shows Orlando capable of knowing both men and women better. Like the female Orlando, Vita had, during her affair with Violet, disguised herself as a man. But I always have the sense that Vita provides the external details for what are, basically, Virginia Woolf's ideas and desires. V. Sackville-West has not written about woman-to-woman relationships as Virginia has. If she has them in mind—as I think she has in *The Edwardians*—Sackville-West treats such relationships very comfortably in male-female terms. We do not know, in short, much of what she thought about specifically womanly friendships. But Virginia has written frequently in her novels, her diary, and *A Room of One's Own* of the necessity for women to recognize their masculine qualities and men their feminine. Otherwise, she feels, the profound differences between the sexes will be further exaggerated and union prevented. What is more, through *Orlando* Virginia Woolf illustrates how one woman may understand her full, androgynous self by coming close to another. The women to whom Orlando feels close—Sasha and the prostitutes—help her find a wider definition of her own womanliness. On another level, the author feels close to Orlando. Virginia Woolf had been attracted to Katherine Mansfield because she had known prostitutes and other women whose life experiences were similarly exotic. Orlando becomes a strong, widely experienced woman, in some respects like, yet more likeable than, the hardened Katherine Mansfield.

As the nineteenth century approaches England, Orlando grows more and more into her womanliness. She begins to pick up something of that century's sense of coupleness and family. Like Vita, Orlando feels just enough of the spirit of her age to survive in society. Though she is naturally an adventurous sort, seeking life and lovers rather than a husband and domesticity, Orlando now yields to Victorianism and seeks a mate. In this way Virginia Woolf explains the situation of a woman like Vita who found the details of family life cloying in the extreme and yet married happily. I have already looked at the independence allowed her in her marriage to Harold Nicolson. For Orlando, Virginia Woolf provides another such marvelously suited husband. Every bit as romantic as his name, Marmaduke Bonthrop Shelmerdine caters to her moods as fast as they succeed each other. He encourages her passionate romantic attitudes; he plays to her acquiescent, quiet periods; and he leaves her to solitude whenever she needs it. They understand each other so well that each thinks the other may be of his own sex. Ugly Harriet, the Roumanian Archduchess, had been fraudulently androgynous: a man dressed, and dressed awkwardly, in women's clothing. He would not have done as a husband for Orlando.

Shelmerdine may be a fantasy husband—even his likeness in the book is taken from an anonymous, brightly colored painting, still hanging at Sissinghurst, of a romantic young man—but there are hints of Harold Nicolson about him. Shelmerdine's nature is mentally androgynous. One of Orlando's names for him, Mar, is a pet name used by the Nicolsons. Furthermore Shelmerdine, though an influential presence in Orlando's life, is actually away most of the time, as Harold Nicolson was before he resigned from the diplomatic service. But Marmaduke Bonthrop Shelmerdine is more like someone Orlando creates for her own purposes than like a real husband. His name and the imagery associated with it at the end of the book—glittering feathers—come to suggest the wild goose which Orlando has been pursuing with her net of words all her life.

Orlando may feel fulfilled on some level through her marriage and the birth of a son, but her more complex self wants desperately to write poetry. To accomplish this end, she needs to be unusually involved with herself. That is how we last see Orlando: she is trying to summon up a coherent picture of herself, composed of all the broken fragments in the book, in order to make another leap for the wild goose. Once again the external details are Vita's and the ideas a merging of Virginia's with what she imagines the created Vita's to be. Orlando receives The Burdett Coutts Memorial Prize for the simple nature poem she has been refining out of her experience for centuries. The Burdett Coutts is Vita's Hawthornden. But Orlando's thoughts about following the gleam, as Tennyson would have it, are expressed in imagery resembling what Virginia had used to explain her own mystical reason for writing. Orlando thinks about the wild goose: "Always it flies fast out to sea and always I fling after it words like nets. . . . And sometimes there's an inch of silver—six words —in the bottom of the net. But never the great fish who lives in the coral groves." Virginia writes in her diary: "It is not oneself but something in the universe that one's left with. It is this that is frightening and exciting in the midst of my profound gloom, depression, boredom, whatever it is. One sees a fin passing far out. . . . But by writing I don't reach anything" (30 September 1926). Orlando also expresses Virginia Woolf's disdain, as she spelled it out in *Three Guineas,* for that modern phenomenon the professional critic of literature, that inflated man who toadies to the writers and condescends to the readers.

Orlando is most nobly infused with Woolf ideas when Orlando calls upon herself and receives in reply the images of the multiple selves she has been, and therefore is. Just as Virginia Woolf addresses the "present owner of the name," her future self at age fifty (in her diary entry for 9 March 1920), and everywhere in the diary addresses a younger Virginia, so Orlando calls upon some of the selves, some of the "incongruous strands," we have seen. Many of the selves are identifiable with traits and experiences of Vita's. Orlando is snobbish about her family and home; she is truthful, generous, and spoiled; she has written some pieces which are romantic and facile: she has a passion for dogs, trees, peasant life, and night; she has loved both men and women. Virginia Woolf has spun these strands together, added certain emanations from herself, and pushed her necessarily incomplete work of art onto the stage at that terrifying time, the present moment: "the emerging monster," as she calls that moment in *The Waves,* "to whom we are attached."

So ends a book which could only have been written by an audacious genius. Like Lily Briscoe, Virginia Woolf had had her vision. She must have felt strangely close to Vita, for the Jessamy Brides had between them created Orlando. After writing her biography of Roger Fry, Virginia Woolf had a similar thought: "What a curious relation is mine with Roger at this moment—I who have given him a kind of shape after his death. Was he like that? I feel very much in his presence at the moment; as if I were intimately connected with him: as if we together had given birth to this vision of him: a child born of us" (*Diary,* 25 July 1940).

J. W. Graham

Point of View in The Waves:
Some Services of the Style

> *I think I am about to embody at last the exact shapes*
> *my brain holds. What a long toil to reach this*
> *beginning—if* The Waves *is my first work in my own*
> *style.* —A Writer's Diary, p. 176 (16 Nov. 1931)

As early as 1928, Virginia Woolf began to formulate in several essays her conception of a new kind of fiction which would combine elements of drama, poetry, and the novel.[1] Although she had no name for this new form, she saw clearly and stated repeatedly that it could not be called a novel. While she was writing *Orlando*, she twice recorded her certainty that she would never write a novel again;[2] and in the manuscript of *The Waves* she scribbled at one point the following requests: "The author would be glad if the following pages were not read as a novel."[3] After *The Waves* had been published, she looked ahead and recorded her

[1]See J. W. Graham, "The 'Caricature Value' of Parody and Fantasy in *Orlando*," *University of Toronto Quarterly, xxx* (1960-1961), 345–366.

[2]Virginia Woolf, *A Writer's Diary* (London: Hogarth Press, 1953), p. 124 (18 March 1928) and p. 128 (31 May 1928). Subsequent references appear in my text in parentheses, after the quotation.

[3]The Manuscript of *The Waves*, v, 208. The permission to quote from this manuscript granted by the estate of the late Leonard Woolf, and to thank the authorities of the Henry W. and Albert A. Berg Collection of the New York Public Library, Astor, Lennox and Tilden Foundations, for permission to publish these quotations.

J. W. Graham, "Point of View in The Waves: *Some Services of the Style,"* University of Toronto Quarterly, *39 (April 1970), pp. 193–211. Reprinted by permission of the author and University of Toronto Press.*

intention to "write another four novels: *Waves,* I mean" (p. 178, 13 Jan. 1932); as if to say that, since this new form of fiction had no proper name of its own, she would call it, for her own purposes, by the name of the work which was her first attempt to create it on a large scale. All this evidence only verifies what the test of *The Waves* makes manifest on every page—that it is a radically a-novelistic work of fiction and that attempts to regard it as a novel will yield very little. For this reason, such critical terms as "plot," "character," and "setting" are the wrong instruments for exploring its nature as fiction.

But the term "point of view," so common in discussions of the novel, is of course still relevant, simply because *The Waves* is a narrative. In the present discussion, I shall analyze the point of view in this work, tracing its gradual development through two holograph drafts and concentrating on the ways in which it is finally established through the agency of style.

In the episodes[4] of *The Waves,* Virginia Woolf rigorously follows two conventions for rendering direct speech: the use of "said" to indicate a speaker, and the use of quotation marks to set off the speech itself. Although these familiar conventions may lead us to assume that we are to hear the dialogue of the speakers, a page or two is enough to make us realize that even the most precocious children would never talk like this. Because Virginia Woolf makes no attempt to distinguish the style of one speaker from that of any other, it is difficult to read the speeches as stream-of-consciousness; and this difficulty is increased when we perceive that the rhythm, sentence structure, and vocabulary of any one speaker do not change noticeably between childhood and middle age. Yet most critics approach *The Waves* as an example of stream-of-consciousness writing. Melvin Friedman describes the method as internal monologue; but the style does not satisfy his insistence that internal monologue must express a character's identity in "words and syntactical

---

The manuscript consists of seven bound volumes and a small looseleaf notebook which pertains to the second draft. The pagination used in this article has been supplied by the authorities of the Berg Collection: each volume is numbered separately, starting with the title page. The seven volumes contain two complete holograph drafts, the first running from Vol. I to p. 76 of Vol. IV, the second to p. 43 of Vol. VII. To my knowledge, no one has preserved the typed revisions to which Virginia Woolf refers in *A Writer's Diary*.

All passages quoted have been edited to remove cancelled words and to incorporate interlinear and marginal revisions. Subsequent references will appear in my text in parentheses, following the quotation, with a roman numeral to signify the volume number, followed by an arabic numeral for the page number.

[4]This term will be used to refer to those sections of the book which deal with the six characters.

units proper to his mentality."[5] Robert Humphrey defines the method as soliloquy, which seems closer to the mark because that is what Virginia Woolf called it; and yet it does not follow his rule that soliloquy must "communicate emotions and ideas which are related to the plot and action."[6] These soliloquies *are* the plot and action of *The Waves,* and if they render anything, it is surely the psychic life of the speakers, the communication of which Humphrey assigns to internal monologue. Both of these critics are searching in their analysis of the methods used in fiction which render a stream of consciousness. It is perhaps more fruitful to assume that *The Waves* is simply not this kind of fiction than to assume that their analysis is at fault.

The most striking departure from prevailing narrative convention is the handling of verb tenses. For most of the book, the characters speak in the pure present (I go), a form of the present tense which we rarely use in speech or thought, in both of which the progressive form (I am going) is far more natural. When we do make use of the pure present, it is chiefly to convey two kinds of activity. The first is an action that is external but has no necessarily fixed location in time, as when we give a recipe, or when we describe actions which are habitual and so are repeated in time. The second is an activity that is internal, such as "I believe," "I feel," and so on—activity exempt from any necessary fixed duration or location in time. In both of these instances, the pure present can be used, as Susanne Langer puts it, to "create the impression of an act, yet suspend the sense of time in regard to it."[7]

Indeed, when it is used to convey an habitual or repeatable act, the pure present does something more subtle than *suspend* our sense of time. As Langer points out, the pure present can convey an external action *as it occurs* only if the action is momentary. When it is used to represent external actions, therefore, it makes them seem momentary, no matter what their actual duration might be in life: they happen so rapidly that we feel them recede into the past even as they occur, and we assume an unconscious mental posture which inclines towards the future. It is probably for these reasons that, in life, we rarely find the pure present a natural form in which to recount actions as they occur, for it seems to rob them of their psychological substance, their felt duration *as actions.*

Yet it is consistently used to narrate such actions in *The Waves.* Consider, for example, this passage with Susan in her kitchen:

[5]Melvin J. Friedman, *Stream of Consciousness: A Study in Literary Method* (New Haven: Yale University Press, 1955), pp. 35–36.

[6]Robert Humphrey, *Stream of Consciousness in the Modern Novel* (Berkeley and Los Angeles: University of California Press, 1955), p. 5.

[7]Susanne Langer, *Feeling and Form* (New York: Scribner, 1953), p. 267.

> I go then to the cupboard, and take the damp bags of rich sultanas; I lift the heavy flour on to the clean scrubbed kitchen table. I knead; I stretch; I pull, plunging my hands into the warm inwards of the dough. I let the cold water stream fanwise through my fingers.[8]

The following remarks may seem excessively ingenious if we limit their relevance to this passage alone; but they are intended, of course, to apply to the cumulative effect of all those parts of *The Waves* in which the pure present is the dominant tense—that is, to the greater part of it, with the exception of the interludes and Bernard's summing up. I have chosen this passage with Susan as an illustration because every verb in it renders an external action.

The scene is marked by an intensity that seems out of proportion to what happens in it—the simple act of making, shall we say, raisin bread. If we transpose the passage into the past tense, it seems like a more natural narrative:

> I went then to the cupboard and took the damp bag of rich sultanas. I lifted the heavy flour on to the clean scrubbed kitchen table. I kneaded, stretched, pulled, plunging my hands into the warm inwards of the dough. I let the cold water stream fanwise through my fingers.

In this version, Susan sounds as if she were giving a methodical minute account of her past actions, much as she might if she had mislaid something and were trying to find it by recalling the detailed sequence of her actions. The urgency has vanished and the passage reads more slowly than it does in the pure present. It seems more natural to eliminate some of the first person pronouns in this version, as I have done; but if we try this with the pure present, the verbs rapidly take on an imperative tone. If we wish to keep the pure present verbs as descriptions of real actions, we must therefore go on repeating the "I" with nearly every one of them: there is no helpful copula, like the "am" of the present progressive "I am going," to keep in our minds a clear notion of the person performing this present action. In the transposed version, the heavy sprinkling of verbs merely makes us feel that Susan is indeed recalling her actions with minute accuracy; but in the original version, the rush of verbs conveys rapidity of the actions themselves.

The second major use of the pure present in life—to convey internal states of mind exempt from any particular duration—profoundly affects the discourse of *The Waves*. We have seen how, in Susan's kitchen, we

[8]Virginia Woolf, *The Waves* (New York: Harcourt, Brace, 1959), p. 99. Subsequent references appear in my text in parentheses, after the quotation.

are struck by the way in which she gives her own physical actions such strenuous scrutiny, and how the impression of close self-scrutiny rises largely from the effects of the pure present. The cumulative effect of this is to bestow on *all* the activities narrated in *The Waves,* whether internal or external, the aura of a meditating mind. The actions of Susan are past, whether in the past of a few moments ago or of years ago; and what is *present* is Susan's *awareness* of her actions. This awareness becomes, through the uniformity of style, not only her own but also that of an invisible narrating consciousness closely resembling the speaker of lyric poetry, in which the pure present is the prevailing tense.

Both these effects of the pure present are continually being created by the peculiar kind of discourse used in *The Waves.* Despite the urgency of the speech, the actions it recounts are not as immediate as we might first expect in a present-tense narrative: they seem to be witnessed at one remove, as if through a reversed telescope which makes them distant though distinct. An air of mysterious significance emanates from them, and the speakers, we feel, are narrating them under some obscure compulsion. Each speaker in *The Waves* steps forward in turn to recount, for his own and for our contemplation, his remembrance of his sensations, actions, memories, thoughts, and feelings, none of which is rendered mimetically. Because the consciousness of all the speakers are rendered in the same style, the cumulative effect is like listening to a running verbatim translation of speeches by six different speakers: the subject matter alters, the attitudes of the speakers vary, they have their characteristic images and expressions, which the translater faithfully mirrors; but the words we actually *hear* are his, and are strongly colored by the nuances and rhythms of his own vocabulary and voice. In the published text of *The Waves*, the translator appears explicitly only in the use of the word "said," which implies that someone is reporting the speeches, and in the interludes, which do not occur in the mind of any character and so must either be interpolations by an omniscient author or direct reflections by the translator as he turns away from the characters and examines the natural world around them.

These faint vestiges are all that remain of a narrator with whom the book started, and who remained explicitly and prominently in it through most of the first draft.

Long before the manuscript was begun, while she was still revising *To the Lighthouse,* Virginia Woolf recorded in her diary her desire to write a "semi-mystic very profound life of a woman, which shall all be told on one occasion; and time shall be utterly obliterated; future shall somehow blossom out of the past" (p. 102, 23 Nov. 1926). In a footnote to this passage Leonard Woolf suggests that it refers to the book which became *The Waves,* and later entries bear him out. Three months later, she noted the possibility of writing "a new kind of play," which would be "away from facts; free; yet concentrated; prose yet poetry; a novel and a play" (p. 104, 21 Feb. 1927); and her rough sketch of this proposed work pictures a man and a woman who think, speak, act, write, and sing in it. During the writing of *Orlando,* she amplified this sketch, casually postulating a narrator and referring to what is narrated as either thought or speech (p. 108, 18 June 1927).

For nearly a year, Virginia Woolf struggled to retain certain advantages offered by a narrator and to diminish the disadvantages, which were enormous. At one point she remarked that she was "not satisfied . . . with the frame" (p. 142, 28 March 1929); and two months after this entry, she clarified the reasons for her dissatisfaction: "But who is she? I am very anxious that she should have no name. I don't want a Lavinia or a Penelope: I want 'she.' But that becomes arty, Liberty greenery yallery somehow: symbolic in loose robes. Of course I can make her think backwards and forwards; I can tell stories. But that's not it" (p. 143, 28 May 1929). Despite the fact that the narrator could move backwards and forwards through time, and could tell various stories, such a figure imposed a rigidity of perspective on the book which a free movement through time would not eliminate; and the problem of giving her some identity, yet leaving her unnamed, meant that Virginia Woolf was bothered by the usual problem of a first-person narrator—that of making her a person vivid enough to be present in the book, yet neutral enough to avoid becoming its center of interest.

The problem did not vanish with concentrated work on the manuscript, which was started on 2 July 1929 (I, p. 1). Three times between this date and 23 September, Virginia Woolf scrapped her draft material and began again from the beginning. Two days after the latter date, she referred tersely to the most pressing of the many problems which confronted her: "Who thinks it? And am I outside the thinker? One wants a device that is not a trick" (p. 146, 25 Sept. 1929). By the end of October, still dissatisfied, she wrote at some length about the same problem: "Is there some falsity of method, somewhere? Something tricky?—so that the interesting things aren't firmly based? I am in an odd state; feel a cleavage; here's my interesting thing; and there's no quite solid table on which to put it. It might come in a flash, on rereading—some solvent. I am convinced that I am right to seek for a station whence I can set my people against time and the sea" (p. 149, 2 Nov. 1929). One function of the narrator was apparently to provide a point of view or "station" from which the characters would be "set" against a background; and yet the narrator did not provide a clear point of view (a "solid table") from which to view the "interesting thing."

When we examine the first draft of *The Waves* we can see why. The first few pages are written from an omniscient point of view, although the style changes rapidly from a lyrical description of the house and the beach to a fantastic description of babies playing on the beach, to an impersonal matter-of-fact description of the individual children. The narrator is sketched in as a vague meditative figure, whose sex is carefully disguised and who speaks briefly in the first person. Although most of the narrative is impersonal, and could be written from the point of view of either the narrator or the author, the narrator is established so uncertainly that we tend to assume an authorial point of view. At times, however, we are suddenly jolted into the realization that it is meant to be that of the narrator. After an omniscient narration of the incident of Jinny kissing Louis in the garden, for example, the narrator suddenly intrudes: "I am not laying too great a stress upon all this. I am not exaggerating the intensity of children's feelings! Indeed, there is nothing more certain than that children are tortured by jealousy and love long before they know their own names; *the mind* was certain of this" (I, p. 27). [Italics mine.] The last clause of this passage suddenly shifts us from the narrator's to the author's point of view, as if Virginia Woolf felt the need to remind us that there *is* a narrator. As the manuscript developed, the narrator grew progressively dim, yet Virginia Woolf continued now and then to refer to this undefined anonymous "mind." It is not surprising that she wondered "who thinks the book?" and whether or not she herself was to be distinct from the speaker.

One effect of this intrusive author-narrator is an extreme detachment from the speakers, whom the reader is led to examine rather as if they were material for a case book. Throughout the first manuscript volume, running from 2 July to 28 October 1929, they scarcely ever speak in the first person. The account of their lives begins with a clinically detached omniscient analysis, of which the following will serve as an example. It is the first attempt to write the visit of Susan and Bernard (here called Johnnie) to Elvedon.

> they communicated to each other some criticism. I am not at all happy, was the gist of what Susan said. I have just seen Jinny kiss Louis. Then Johnnie said that it was unreasonable to expect entire happiness. But nobody was wicked. And he described Jinny's character very cleverly. He made phrases about her and Louis; as he had about the fly and the spider. Susan was

> distracted by these phrases, and said that she supposed John would be an artist, a maker of phrases. And they saw the lady writing; and her conservatory; and John described it all, even though it was before their eyes; a curious habit; and also they imagined the lady's life, and her character, and how she was writing to her lover, no; she was too old; to her sailor son who was beyond the sea.
>
> The point of the story is the phrasemaking. For the sake of them, Susan liked going with John; but better still she liked to adventure all day into the heart of the wind (I, pp. 29–31).

This condensed scenario, written consistently in the past tense, is followed by an abstract oracular analysis of what Elvedon means to the children, written in the present tense:

> Here was the beginning, here was the first writing on the page. The woods of Elvedon are seen through the soul; and life is mixed with other lives; and the mind is haunted with the figure of a lady, writing, between two windows. And the solitary is no longer solitary; and the mind, like a vine, has forever now to find a phrase to net things in; for otherwise they must perish. And then, when the phrase has been found, it must be spoken aloud, to somebody else (I, p. 33).

By the time she finished the first volume of her manuscript, Virginia Woolf had begun to intensify these analytical passages, as in this scene with Rhoda in the schoolroom:

> Suddenly, as she closed the loop of the figure six, she had a visitation of appalling solemnity. She heard time beating; she heard the world outside continuing its enormous existence, with complete indifference to her own shrunken body, sitting at the table. There it all was, in the loop; and all power of movement had been [illegible word]; and being outside the world, her movements were indifferent, she had no existence; she was like a leaf blown about; and all was vain; and withered; and accidental; and nothing that anybody could do had any importance (I, p. 169).

Here the prose rhythm is beginning to approach the urgency of the text, and the imagery is far more intense than in the passages quoted above; but the point of view remains completely omniscient. On the rare occasions when someone speaks in the first person, he speaks briefly, and we are instantly told that "Rhoda thought" this, or that this was how Jinny or Susan "felt." At times this produces passages of extreme awkwardness; and in one of these we see how strongly Virginia Woolf tended to retain the omniscient point of view. It deals with Bernard at college:

> I am one of those people whose lives will never be altogether satisfactory
> because there is a certain inevitable disparity between my public self and my
> private self—between the outer and the inner. Bernard said this to himself;
> returning from a party; he was at college; and he had come back, very late,
> to his own rooms; and his thought, though not spoken aloud, yet preserved,
> even in his mind, something of the roundness and explicitness which words
> bestow (II, p. 75).

Here Bernard is allowed only to utter his thoughts: we are then *told* that
they were his thoughts and are *told* his actions. The clumsiness of this,
with its approach to and retreat from Bernard's consciousness, is surprising in view of the skills Virginia Woolf had developed in writing *Mrs.
Dalloway* and *To the Lighthouse*. It was written nearly six months after
she had begun her manuscript, months in which she had given close
attention to her book and had repeatedly expressed her uneasiness about
the way it was going.

   Not until she had begun to write the first draft of the farewell dinner
party, on 3 January 1930 (II, p. 189), did the characters speak in a way
resembling the published text. Even here, the first draft tends at the
beginning of the scene to relapse into the third person; and when it
develops into a "conversation" among the characters, we realize that it is
intended to be actual dialogue, not the speech of minds. It was shortly
after starting this scene that Virginia Woolf recorded in the diary her
feeling that she had broken through some barrier (p. 152, 12 Jan. 1930);
and it seems likely that her sudden sense of liberation was connected with
the virtual abandonment of the narrator's omniscient interventions, which
from this point on occur only when the actions of the characters must be
rendered, and even then with diminishing frequency. Not until August
1930, however, three months after she had started on the second draft,
did Virginia Woolf record her feeling that *The Waves* was "resolving
itself . . . into a series of dramatic soliloquies" (p. 159, 20 Aug. 1930).

   For three and a half years—from the diary reference in June 1926 to
the first draft of the farewell dinner—Virginia Woolf imagined and tried
to establish a narrator's point of view in *The Waves*. The significant
points about this struggle are that it occurred at all and that it went on for
so long. By the time she wrote *The Waves,* Virginia Woolf was a
professional who had written six novels, two of them marked by an
impressive skill in manipulating point of view; yet she tried at length to
establish a point of view in *The Waves* that could only produce more
difficulties than advantages. The narrator could not take her place in the
narrative among the other speakers because she is omniscient and they
most certainly are not; for the same reason, her presence could not

establish the air of immediacy which is one of the advantages of first-person narration; and again for the same reason, she could not be dramatized, like the narrator in *The Turn of the Screw*. Referred to constantly as "the lonely mind," and described in carefully vague terms, the narrator could not acquire any identity in the reader's mind, and could become a real presence in the book only by intruding into the story.

But Virginia Woolf was a precise artist, and *The Waves* is her most laboriously wrought book; so that the struggle with the point of view in the early stages of composition can only mean that, although there were obvious reasons for abandoning the narrator, there were less obvious but potent reasons for trying to keep her.

The "method" for which Virginia Woolf had earned her reputation by 1929 was marked by the pervasive stylistic presence of the author as narrator, despite her desire to eliminate herself as narrator and to render the luminous halo of consciousness worn by each of her characters. Why, then, did she engage in this long struggle to incorporate into *The Waves* a first-person narrator, when it would seem that her purposes might be served just as well by writing from the point of view which she had mastered so well? The answer must be, that her purposes could no longer be served by her established method, and that she had a powerful motive for seeking to make certain features of a first-person narrative the controlling point of view in this book.

I suggest that the root reasons for establishing this elaborately indirect point of view in *The Waves* are buried in the seminal experience out of which the book grew. This occurred in the fall of 1926, at Rodmell, while Virginia Woolf was revising *To the Lighthouse;* at which time she recorded it in her diary:

> I wish to add some remarks to this, on the mystical side of this [solitude]; how it is not oneself but something in the universe that one's left with. It is this that is frightening and exciting in the midst of my profound gloom, depression, boredom, whatever it is. One sees a fin passing far out. What image can I reach to convey what I mean? Really there is none, I think. The interesting thing is that in all my feeling and thinking I have never come up against this before. Life is, soberly and accurately, the oddest affair; has in it the essence of reality. I used to feel this as a child—couldn't step across a puddle once, I remember, for thinking how strange—what am I? etc. But by writing I don't reach anything. All I mean to make is a note of a curious state of mind. I hazard the guess that it may be the impulse behind another book. [9]

[9] *A Writer's Diary*, pp. 101–102, (30 Sept. 1926). Mr. Leonard Woolf kindly verified this passage against the manuscript of the diary, and reported that, owing to a misprint, the word "solicitude" in the first sentence should read "solitude."

Immediately after completing the first draft of *The Waves,* she remarked
that "this is a reach after that vision I had, the unhappy summer—or three
weeks—at Rodmell, after finishing the *Lighthouse*" (p. 158, 29 April
1930). And nine months later, a few minutes after finishing the second
draft, she evaluated her effort by saying, "I mean that I have netted that
fin in the waste of water which appeared to me over the marshes out of my
window at Rodmell when I was coming to an end of *To the Lighthouse*" (p.
169, 7 Feb. 1931).

In the text of *The Waves,* the vision of a fin in a waste of water is
given in its most extended form to Bernard, when he is in Rome undergo-
ing one of his rare moments of detachment, during which Time, as he
puts it (p. 184), tapers to a point and discharges a drop, a distillation of
experience which runs down the walls of his mind and changes his
perspective. These moments, he says just before he narrates this one, are
the "true events."

> Leaning over this parapet I see far out a waste of water. A fin turns. This
> bare visual impression is unattached to any line of reason, it springs up as
> one might see the fin of a porpoise on the horizon. Visual impressions often
> communicate thus briefly statements that we shall in time to come uncover
> and coax into words. I note under F., therefore, 'Fin in a waste of waters.' I,
> who am perpetually making notes in the margin of my mind for some final
> statement, make this mark, waiting for some winter's evening.
>
> Now I shall go and lunch somewhere, I shall hold my glass up, I shall
> look through the wine, I shall observe with more than my usual detachment,
> and when a pretty woman enters the restaurant and comes down the room
> between the tables I shall say to myself, Look where she comes against a
> waste of waters. A meaningless observation, but to me, solemn, state-
> coloured, with a fatal sound of ruining worlds and waters falling to destruc-
> tion (p. 189).

In his summing up, when he does make his final statement on a winter's
evening, Bernard recalls a critical experience of his life and remembers
how he "cried with a sudden conviction of complete desertion, now there
is nothing. No fin breaks the waste of this immeasurable sea. Life has
destroyed me" (p. 284). Even at the time she recorded it, Virginia Woolf
did not feel that the image of a fin in a waste of waters (or any other
image) could convey what she meant; and it is reasonable to assume that,
whatever it meant at that time, a great deal more naturally emerged in the
complex process of creating *The Waves.* Yet her ritualistic gesture
towards the source of the book after she had finished each draft makes it
clear that for four and a half years this experience remained for her the
gauge by which she measured her success. For that reason alone it
demands attention, however circumspect.

Those aspects of the experience most relevant to the present discussion of style have to do not with what the vision "meant" but with certain qualitative elements of the experience itself, elements revealed in the way she spoke of it in the diary entry quoted above. The first of these is the *radically* contemplative nature of the experience. The vision came unsolicited, suddenly intruding on a prevailing mood of gloomy depression and boredom; and although she refers to it as "frightening and exciting," the manner in which she records it is notably unshaken. Her alert detachment may stem from the fact that it constituted no threat to her personally: indeed, her role seems to have been that of an attentive spectator watching something "far out," remote from her own person. The emotions she felt were not about herself but about "something in the universe that one's left with." In no sense was the vision the result of any kind of effort on her part, and her personal remoteness from the whole experience is manifest in her skeptical conclusion that it may have been nothing more than "a curious state of mind." In the same way, Bernard's strange detachment from the ordinary flow of life comes unsought; he wishes it would end; he cannot understand at the time what his vision of the fin means; and he disposes of it as quickly as he can, filing it away in his mind for future reference. The fear and excitement felt by Virginia Woolf were virtually impersonal, more like attributes of the thing seen than emotional responses of the seer. In both her case and Bernard's, the experience is marked by an absence of violent response, by an alert wondering passivity, by an inability to explain the meaning of the vision, and by a rapt detachment.

When we reflect on these features of the seminal vision out of which *The Waves* grew, it is easier to perceive why Virginia Woolf's established method was, from her point of view, no longer adequate. With the contemplative detachment of the vision had gone a corollary surrender to what is contemplated—a submission that was uncritical, responsive, passive; in a very real sense an impersonal recognition of something moving "far out." But her famous method had been designed to immerse the reader in the personality of the character, so that he viewed events from within, discerning no more than the character discerns, and achieving his detachment from the character mainly through symbolic detail and structural juxtapositions.

I have elsewhere [10] discussed Virginia Woolf's growing dissatisfaction, in the years immediately preceding *Orlando,* with what she called "psychology"; her desire to break free from "personality" as the subject of her fiction; and her determination to achieve in her fiction the impersonality she associated with poetry. The method she had developed

[10]Graham, "The 'Caricature Value' of Parody and Fantasy in *Orlando.*"

trapped her in the personality of her characters, so that any sense of "something in the universe one's left with" was almost inevitably rendered as felt by a character—Clarissa's vision of the old lady across the way, or Mrs. Ramsay's vision of the lighthouse—rather than as a feeling generated in the reader by the narrative itself. On the other hand, direct authorial omniscience imposes on the reader a detachment that is necessarily critical, analytical, and evaluative, because the omniscience of an omniscient author is constantly assumed by the reader even when it is not explicitly asserted. We recognize in *Middlemarch,* for example, certain forces at work of which the characters are unaware, and our recognition is intellectual in nature, a form of *knowledge* superior to theirs because it is established for us by the omniscient author-narrator. In contrast to this effect of authorial omniscience, the narrative continuum that Virginia Woolf sought to establish might be termed omnipercipience: a *perception* (not an understanding) of the characters' inner experience fused with a *perception* (not an understanding) of what they do not perceive—the background of time and the sea against which they are set.

The sketches of the narrator in the early stages of the manuscript are illuminating in this connection. She defines her role quite explicitly on one occasion: "I am the seer. I am the force that arranges. I am the thing in which all this exists. Certainly without me it would perish. I can give it order. I perceive what is bound to happen" (I, p. 38). Exempt from the condition of time which restricts the children, she perceives what is bound to happen; but she does not make it happen. As she sits staring into the folds of a napkin which become waves breaking on the beach, she recounts minutely everything called up by her vatic power—the appearance, gestures, thoughts, speeches of the children, as well as the panorama of the natural world to which she turns now and then. But she is not making up a story, she is telling one that has existed from the beginning of time.

In the opening pages of the first draft of *The Waves* there is another passage in which the narrator meditates not on her role or her power, but on her purpose:

> I am telling myself the story of the world from the beginning. I am not concerned with the single life, but with lives together. I am trying to find, in the folds of the past, such fragments as time, having broken the perfect vessel, still keeps safe. The perfect vessel? But it was not by any means made of durable stuff. For it was only when the thing had happened and the violence of the shock was over that one could understand, or really live; only when one had left the room and was walking home at dead of night. Then in that darkness, which had no limit, very dark, whose shores were

> invisible, whatever had happened, expanded; and something dropped
> away. Then, without a companion, one loved; spoke with no one to hear;
> and carried on an intercourse with people who were not there more com-
> pletely than [when] one's chair was drawn close to theirs (I, p. 17).

The narrator's search for the fragments of the perfect vessel controls
her entire relation to the narrative, making it a quest; and her quest forces
her to scrutinize intensely everything which is called up from the past. As
we have seen, the feeling of closely examining the events of the narrative
is created in the reader by the use of the pure present; and the reader's
relation to the narrative is uncontrollably though subtly colored by this
ambience of search, longing, and (by implication) loss.

In the same manuscript passage, still more is revealed about our
relation to the narrator, and therefore to her narration. The first statement
she makes—"I am telling myself"—establishes the fact that she is
talking and that she is not talking to us. We are eavesdroppers, overhear-
ing her story; and because she is not aware of us, she is free simply to
recount her story, free to pursue what interests her, free from any
obligation to provide us with any knowledge about the narrative. Her next
statement—"the story of the world from the beginning"—makes it clear
that we are not going to hear a story about the speaker, who is dealing
with *the* world, not *her* world. It also makes it clear that her story is about
the past, which she has the power to call up in minute detail.

In one of her early notes on *The Waves,* already quoted, Virginia
Woolf referred to the problem of giving her narrator identity yet keeping
her nameless, and added the acid warning to herself: "But that becomes
arty, Liberty greenery yallery somehow: symbolic in loose robes" (p.
143, 28 May 1929). The warning revealed as much about her purpose as
her danger. The narrator had to be a seer, a visionary; she had to wear the
robes of the *vates* in some sense; and this was so far removed from
contemporary conventions that Virginia Woolf could pinpoint ironically
the risk involved in creating such a figure. As a figure distinctly intruding
between the reader and the narrative in the first draft, the narrator was
indeed oracular and pompous. But even when the narrator becomes so
attenuated that few readers suspect her existence, her bardic voice continues to deliver the book, employing many weapons from the bard's
armory: rhythm used for hypnotic effect and to control emotional pitch;
the structural use of recurrent images and symbols; abrupt transitions in
time and place; a free movement back and forth among the characters and
events of the narrative; repetition used deliberately for incantatory effect;
a heavy use of appositions (one might almost call them kennings); and at
all times, the tireless driving voice, ranging in tone from the antiphonal

solemnity of the dinner scenes to the quiet directness of some parts of Bernard's summing-up, but never relaxing into the idiom of colloquial discourse.

Because this voice is speaking to itself, the lyric effects of waking dream, the visionary flight, are possible. Virginia Woolf habitually used "speaks" and "thinks" interchangeably when speculating about *The Waves*, [11] and this synonymous use of two very different words shows how persistently she aimed at a blend of both. When the *speaking* voice is stressed, the discourse takes on the tone of bardic delivery; when the *thinking* voice is stressed, it assumes the more intimate tone of lyric meditation. At no time is it truly dramatic, except, perhaps, when we first begin to read it and are deceived by the illusion of direct address.

This examination has been directed at the fundamental way in which this speech peculiar to *The Waves* governs the reader's relation to the entire book. It *seems* that he is present in the consciousness of each character at the moment when the psychic action occurs; but he is actually stationed close to—not *in*—an omniscient consciousness which recounts to itself, without comment, the consciousnesses of six speakers, each of whom is talking (or thinking) to himself about his own experience.

When the containing consciousness in which *The Waves* takes place examines the inner life of the six speakers, it is examining itself: they are not meant to be "human beings" but figures who act out the dilemma of consciousness for its own enlightenment. Shortly before the book was published, Virginia Woolf told her husband that the *dramatis personae* were meant to be "severally facets of a single complete person." [12] At the psychological level, the speakers are incarnations of various aspects of the individual soul of the narrating Consciousness, and the psychological traits they possess are called into play by the search which she conducts, through them, for the fragments of the perfect vessel hidden in time past. The informing energy of the book is the longing which compels them to this search, and this longing suffuses the narrative through the stylistic features I have examined. In the meditation quoted above, the narrator concludes that "it was only when the thing had happened and the violence of the shock was over that one could understand." Only the past yields to understanding; and understanding no longer comes in miraculous revelations like those which came to Septimus, Clarissa, Mrs. Ramsay, and Lily Briscoe. If the moment of being—the perfect vessel—is to come at all, it must be patiently recovered, as the result of a sustained visionary search. Most of the events in *The Waves* are colored by this

---

[11]See *A Writer's Diary*, p. 104 (21 Feb. 1927), p. 108 (18 June 1927), pp. 142–143 (28 May 1929), p. 153 (26 Jan. 1930), p. 156 (28 March 1930).

[12]Leonard Woolf, "Virginia Woolf and 'The Waves,' " *The Listener*, No. 136, 1755 (28 June 1957), 25.

unremittent labor of contemplation, so that even the simplest sensory impressions, as we have seen in the case of Susan cooking, are charged with the tension of sifting all experience for the fragments of reality.

But this dominant tension shifts subtly in the final section, Bernard's summing-up. While she was writing the first draft, Virginia Woolf remarked that she could not guess how the book would end, and then added, "It might be a gigantic conversation" (p. 153, 26 Jan. 1930). Two months later, she elaborated on this when she reflected, "How to end, save by a tremendous discussion, in which every life shall have its voice—a mosaic—I do not know" (p. 156, 28 March 1930). She began to work on the final episode only ten days after this entry, and yet there is no sign in the manuscript of any attempt at a conversation in which every life has its voice: instead, she gave all the lives through one voice, Bernard's. There were very good practical reasons for this decision. The cyclical structure from which she never deviated, and which demanded the treatment of old age and death, meant that she could not end the book immediately after the reunion dinner, at which the speakers have reached middle age; and yet to deal with the old age and death of each speaker in turn, as she had so far done with the other stages of their lives, would have meant a much longer book and would still have left unsolved the problem of how to conclude. Whatever the motives for giving the summing-up to one speaker, it is clear that Virginia Woolf's decision to break this prevailing convention of the book, and others as well, subtly altered the reader's relation to what is narrated in the summing-up, and therefore to the work as a whole.

The point of view from which the summing-up is narrated is almost identical with that which had prevailed in the early phases of the manuscript, when the omniscient narrator was still present. Like her, Bernard is telling the story of the world from the beginning; like her, he narrates it in the past tense and comments on it in the present; like her, he is seated at a table with the conscious purpose of recovering from the past such fragments as time, having broken the perfect vessel, still keeps safe; and like her he finds that the scrutiny of his past forces him to deal not with the single life but with lives together. This resemblance points to the structural function of the summing-up. We have seen how, until this point in it is reached, *The Waves* has been a work in which we are confronted not with an image of experience but with an image of its refraction through a narrating consciousness into the prismatic facets of the individual speakers. The summing-up is designed to bring the lives of these partial and shifting figures slowly together, to focus them until, in the last pages of the book, they converge into one burning point of illumination. Its function is analogous to that of the party scene in *Mrs. Dalloway*, where the incidents of the party are meant to "sum up" Clarissa and to focus upon her figure when she suddenly reappears. The urge to gather in the entire book, to epitomize its themes, to raise its emotional pitch to a climactic level at the end and thereby to give the effect of sudden release from its dominant tensions, seems to have compelled Virginia Woolf more powerfully as her career advanced: from *Orlando* on, each work moves towards the final conjunction of vision and fact, a moment in which the disparity between the two vanishes, until, in *Between the Acts,* that conjunction is implicit in the structure of the entire work.

One of the two dominant themes of the summing-up is the communion with his friends—all absent and some dead—which Bernard now enjoys. Because he alone narrates the end of the book, the form of the narrative is a verbal simulacrum of this communion. The most common image of communion is that of one body, of which the communicants are members; and since the only "body" given to the *dramatis personae* of *The Waves* is speech, the one voice of Bernard in the summing-up *is* that body. This may well be the most important single result of having only one speaker in the last episode, because, although it operates slowly and subtly, it allowed Virginia Woolf to ring the changes upon the mysterious identity of Bernard and the others with a freedom which the juxtaposed but isolated soliloquies of the previous episodes had cramped.

To effect this gathering-in of the narrative, it was necessary to release the reader from certain conventions which had established the oblique point of view examined in this essay. The invention of a silent dinner companion breaks the convention that we are listening to a speech uttered by the mind in silence. In the first draft, this obliging nonentity was given a name and a sketchy past; but in her revisions, Virginia Woolf made him more and more shadowy, until in the text he has no identity at all. He is there solely for the purpose of making Bernard's "speech" a form of direct address, delivered across a dinner table to someone known only as "you"—really the reader. Bernard is not engaged in the same sort of uncertain struggle to fathom for *himself* the meaning of his life: he is attempting to articulate this meaning for the silent figure sitting across from him. As a result, we are released from the refracting ambience of consciousness in which we were confined in the previous episodes, so that Bernard's rambling talk feels at once more self-possessed, detached, and spontaneous than the other speeches thus far.

Another change in the dominant conventions of *The Waves* reinforces this tone of naturalness and ease. Because the bulk of the summing-up concerns Bernard's past, the pure present tense rarely appears. The usual tenses are restored: when he narrates his past, he uses the past tense; and when he uses the pure present, it is for the sort of generalizing comment on that past which anyone engaged in a similar process of recollection and evaluation might make. In the other episodes, the quest for meaning was carried on as the speakers were harried by the incessant flood of present moments, from which they escaped only on rare occasions, notably at the two dinners; but Bernard's quest is deliberate and detached as he sets out to stand aside from his life, view it in its totality, and articulate its meaning if he can. His narrative of his past life is not invaded by the present moment, and when at last he returns his attention to the restaurant in which he has been sitting, he refers to the door through which people have been coming and going all through his summing-up, and which symbolized, at the farewell dinner, the rhythmical reiterations of the present moment. "But now let the door open, the glass door that is forever turning on its hinges. Let a woman come, let a young man in evening-dress with a moustache sit down: is there anything that they can tell me? . . . The shock of the falling wave which has sounded all my life . . . no longer makes quiver what I hold" (p. 291).

Standing as it were on higher ground than any he has found through the course of the book, Bernard finds his attention gripped by two recurrent realities in his life: the unending struggle against "those enemies who change but are always there; the forces we fight against" (p. 240); and the growing sense of mysterious identity with his friends. The summing-up is thus structured around the two "streams" or "currents" mentioned in Virginia Woolf's early notes on the book which was to become *The Waves* but which at that time she called *The Moths*. In her diary, she referred to "the idea of some continuous stream, not solely of human thought, but of the ship, the night, etc., all flowing together; intersected by the arrival of the bright moths" (p. 108, 18 June 1927). Almost two years later, when she was beginning intensive work on the book, she referred again to "the stream that I am trying to convey; life itself going on . . . I shall have the two currents—the moths flying along; the flower upright in the centre; a perpetual crumbling and renewing of the plant" (p. 143, 28 May 1929). Eventually, the moths vanished, the title changed, and the recurrent life-death cycle of the motionless flower was replaced by the recurrent rise and fall of the waves. However remote they may seem from the book which finally developed out of them, these early notes reflect the fundamental dramatic opposition between "life itself" and the course taken by its creature, which "intersects," cuts across and counter to, the impersonal rhythm of time—just as the fin turns in a waste of water, following its own course. We have seen how this conflict was embodied in the style of *The Waves,* so that its tensions lend the work an urgency far greater than the bare matter with which it deals would seem to warrant. In the summing-up, however,

Bernard has escaped these tensions as far as his subjective state is concerned, is free to examine them deliberately and calmly, and has discovered something which they cannot undermine, as they have long since undermined the solitary defenses of his private and isolated self-hood.

This discussion began with a description of certain stylistic features of *The Waves* that strike us as unusual: the rigid uniformity of the language throughout and its verbal sophistication, both of which make it unsuitable as vehicle for even one stream of consciousness, much less those of six characters; the heavy use of the pure present tense, which subtly blurs the temporal location and duration of actions, thereby turning them into abstract states of mind; and the constant reiteration of the first-person pronoun, which emphasizes the self-consciousness of the speakers. In analyzing the role played by the narrator in the early stages of the manuscript, I have tried to show that her presence, artistically cumbersome though it may have been, established for the reader a point of view more complex and indirect than at first seems to be the case; that this oblique angle of vision was maintained in the final version of the book through the agency of style; and that this indirection leads the reader to feel the complex quality of Virginia Woolf's vision at Rodmell, with its strange blend of fear and excitement, detachment and involvement, remoteness and intensity, impersonality and rapt absorption.

James Hafley

The Years

The Years—possibly the best, and certainly one of the most interesting, of Virginia Woolf's novels—was published in 1937. It is by far the longest novel after *Night and Day,* and is divided into eleven sections, each of which is subdivided into several parts. The central characters of this novel are the members and friends of the large, upper-middle-class Pargiter family, followed from an afternoon in April, 1880, to a summer night in the "present day"; the setting is England, and for the most part London.

Although *The Years* resembles *The Waves* in certain respects, superficial and essential, it is not true that *The Years* is a repetition of that book,[1] that Virginia Woolf "persists in limiting herself to purely formal variations upon the same old dirge-like tune."[2] Actually, the "tune" here is no more a dirge than it was in any of the preceding novels; there is a formal variation precisely because *The Years* deals with materials ignored by *The Waves.* Like *The Waves, The Years* follows a number of people from youth to age; there are ten relatively short sections, followed by a long "summing up"; the formal perspective is a means of discovering and demonstrating a philosophical perspective that in turn gives

[1]D. S. Savage, "Virginia Woolf," in *The Withered Branch—Six Studies in the Modern Novel* (London: Eyre and Spottiswood, 1950), p. 100.

[2]William Troy, "Variations on a Theme," *Nation* (April 24, 1937), 474. This seems a meaningless comment, and the value judgment it suggests is not substantiated: Shakespeare's tragedies could also be called "formal variations upon the same old . . . tune," for example.

From James Hafley, The Glass Roof, *1954. Originally published by the University of California Press; reprinted by permission of The Regents of the University of California.*

meaning to the characters and circumstance. Descriptions of the weather
begin each section of *The Years,* and such descriptions also begin many
of the subdivisions within each section; of one of these, Wiget writes:
"Die meterologischen Beschreibungen des Frühlings 1880 dehnen sich
gleichzeitig über Stadt und Land aus, wobei ihre Auswirkungen auf das
menschliche Gemüt, in einen lebhaften Rhythmus gebracht, lebhaft vor
den Augen des Lesers entstehen, so dass zwischen Leser und Buch eine
intime Verbindung hergestellt wird."[3] This seems true, although it is
perhaps rather a subjective reaction; a more important function of these
descriptions is to produce a union of apparent opposites within the novel
itself: they serve the same function, but not to the same degree or in
exactly the same manner, as do the descriptive passages of *The Waves.*

Despite these similarities, the differences between the two books are
more important. In *The Years* all that Percival symbolized—all that was
refracted to the reader only through the soliloquies of the readers—is
directly apprehended. In a very limited sense *The Waves* had social
consciousness; *The Years* is dependent for its effect upon immediate and
extensive social consciousness. Moreover, it deals with characters from
every English class; the point of view is more objectively omniscient than
in *The Waves*—so that it tends to approximate dramatic point of view—
and social behavior, instead of exclusive symbolism, prompts and
explains individual response. In *The Waves* there were no direct conversation and no direct description of action; in *The Years* conversation and
behavior are reported at length, and thought transcriptions are both
relatively infrequent and brief.

The Years is concerned with good and evil, right and wrong; it can
be called a justification, from Virginia Woolf's perspective, of the way of
God to men. The death of Percival in *The Waves* was of course a symbol
of evil; in *The Years,* however, there is no such abstraction: evil is
presented not only dramatically but also immediately; good, therefore, is
also presented actively—not simply as "the Good," but as this and that
good behavior in society; *The Years* is a scenic novel, so that the reader
remembers people and action rather than individual mood and attitude.
By "facing the facts"—by managing to surmount the difficulties noted
in Virginia Woolf's criticism of fiction—this novel achieves symbolic
values much more impressive than those in *The Waves,* and much less
dependent upon Bergsonism for their validity.

[3]Erik Wiget, *Virginia Woolf und Die Konzeption der Zeit in ihren Werken* (Zurich: Juris
Verlag, 1949), p. 93. "The meteorological descriptions of spring 1880 extend simultaneously over city and country, whereby their effects on the human mind, rendered in a lively
rhythm, emerge lifelike for the eyes of the reader, so that between reader and book an
intimate bond is created." (*editor's translation*)

> The music stopped. The young man who had been putting records on the gramophone had walked off. The couples broke apart and began to push their way through the door. They were going to eat perhaps; they were going to stream out into the back garden and sit on hard sooty chairs. The music which had been cutting grooves in [Peggy's] mind had ceased. There was a lull—a silence. Far away she heard the sounds of the London night; a horn hooted; a siren wailed on the river. The far-away sounds, the suggestion they brought in of other worlds, indifferent to this world, of people toiling, grinding, in the heart of darkness, in the depths of night, made her say over Eleanor's words, Happy in this world, happy with living people. But how can one be "happy," she asked herself, in a world bursting with misery? On every placard at every street corner was Death; or worse—tyranny; brutality; torture; the fall of civilization; the end of freedom. We here, she thought, are only sheltering under a leaf, which will be destroyed. And then Eleanor says the world is better, because two people out of all those millions are "happy."

This is the central problem of *The Years*. The idea itself is not a new one: although tyranny, loss of freedom, is now the greatest enemy, "Death" brings to mind the closing passage of *The Waves,* and it will be remembered that Clarissa Dalloway felt somehow justified in enjoying her roses and forgetting her husband's concern for the exploited, miserably poor "Albanians, or was it the Armenians?" The earlier novels hinted, in varying degrees, at the existence of the sordid and painful; *The Years* is able to present them directly as part of the immediate scene, and to make its own affirmation all the more convincing by doing so, looking at a wide world rather than an arbitrarily limited one. Again and again throughout the novel sordidity and sublimity are juxtaposed not theoretically but scenically, as they appear in concrete actions and milieus. "The shops were turning into houses; there were big houses and little houses; public houses and private houses. And here a church raised its filigree spire. Underneath were pipes, wires, drains." Both the world above the street and the world below are pictured in this novel, largely in terms of social classes.

> The streets they were driving through were horribly poor; and not only poor . . . but vicious. Here was the vice, the obscenity, the reality of London. It was lurid in the mixed evening light. . . . Parnell. He's dead, Eleanor said to herself, still conscious of the two worlds; one flowing in wide sweeps overhead, the other tip-tapping circumscribed upon the pavement.

For "the night was full of roaring and cursing; of violence and unrest, also of beauty and joy." *The Years,* instead of selecting the beauty and joy for immediate presentation, offers the ugliness and sorrow of the life it depicts side by side with that beauty and joy, in order to justify and order the whole. When Kitty Lasswade goes to hear *Siegfried,* "the music excited her. It was magnificent. Siegfried took the broken pieces of the sword and blew on the fire and hammered, hammered, hammered . . . until at last up he swung the sword high above his head and brought it down—crack! The anvil burst asunder." This refers at once back to Kitty's tea with the Robsons—too poor for her to feel at ease with them, and whose attractive son was hammering, hammering at work when she arrived—and also forward to the sordid flat in which Maggie and Sara Pargiter are spending the same evening. Siegfried's singing has been sublime; but

> "Sing something," said Maggie suddenly. Sara turned and struck the notes.
> "Brandishing, flourishing my sword in my hand . . ." she sang. The words were the words of some pompous eighteenth century march, but her voice was reedy and thin. Her voice broke. She stopped singing.
> She sat silent with her hands on the notes. "What's the good of singing if one hasn't any voice?" she murmured.

And later

> Somebody was hammering on the door of the next house . . . hammer, hammer, hammer. . . .
> "Upcher's come home drunk and wants to be let in," said Maggie. . . .
> A woman's voice was heard shrieking abuse at the man. He bawled back in a thick drunken voice from the doorstep. Then the door slammed.
> They listened.
> "Now he'll stagger against the wall and be sick," said Maggie.

In this way, scene is joined with scene, character juxtaposed with character, until the entire novel is an arrangement of vivid contrasts.

Behind these several contrasts is the gradual decay of Victorian culture, the gradual shift from nineteenth-century "security" to contemporary "confusion," so that those characters who are most aware wonder whether there can be any valid standard, any rule for conduct, in the midst of this continual flux. This social shift finally expresses itself in the contrast between the scene in the Pargiter home at the beginning of the novel and Delia's party at the conclusion—between the Victorian family tea and the sprawling, untidy, crowded group who sit on the floor and drink their soup from mugs; and the change is so depicted that the contrast is finally one between a static, hypocritical society and a dynamic, honest, and energetic if chaotic society.

In this change and flux two things remain constant. The weather is common to good and bad behavior, to beautiful and ugly conduct. As has been said, each section of the novel begins with a description of the weather; and in the scenes following, in which good and evil are violently juxtaposed and mingled, the weather is the same. "Over Park Lane and Piccadilly the clouds kept their freedom . . . staining windows gold, daubing them black. . . ." However—and this paradox has been noted in Virginia Woolf's earlier novels—though the weather is consistent, the weather is always changing: though beneath diversity there is unity, that unity is diversity itself. Thus the weather is a perfect symbol for Virginia Woolf's concept of unity. In exactly the same way the characters of the novel remain constant. However much they may change, age, weaken, they are always the same and always different. The problem of identity, treated in *The Waves,* reappears here, and is given a solution: North thinks:

> Why not down barriers and simplify? But a world, he thought, that was all one jelly, one mass, would be a rice pudding world, a white counterpane world. To keep the emblems and tokens of North Pargiter—the man Maggie laughs at; the Frenchman holding his hat; but at the same time spread out, make a new ripple in human consciousness, be the bubble and the stream, the stream and the bubble—myself and the world together. . . . Anonymously. . . . But what do I mean, he wondered—I, to whom ceremonies are suspect and religion's dead; who don't fit . . . anywhere?

The conclusion of the novel is to answer North's question.

In a review of *The Years* entitled "The End of the English Novel?" J. H. Roberts, praising the book and noting that it had "the utmost technical brilliance," nevertheless felt that Virginia Woolf was ending the life of the novel by saying that no one can know anyone else. The novel, Roberts explained, should teach its readers about other people and illumine life, but he believed Virginia Woolf's theme to be that "we live a riddle . . . we shall never solve the mystery."[4] W. H. Mellers, quoting from the novel itself, calls its theme "the passage of time and its tragedy."[5] Neither of these critics is correct.

[4] J. H. Roberts, "The End of the English Novel?" *Virginia Quarterly Review* (Summer, 1937), 437–439.

[5] W. H. Mellers, "Mrs. Woolf and Life," in Eric Bentley (ed.), *The Importance of Scrutiny,* (New York: George W. Stewart, 1948), p. 380 [Cf. *The Years* (New York: Harcourt, Brace, 1937), p. 184.] Mellers' statement that "the complete omission, in a work which embraces the passage of time during the last fifty years, of (for example) physical desire may strike us at least as odd," is itself odd: in the very first sequence, and throughout the novel, physical desire is dealt with both explicitly and implicity.

> We all think the same things; only we do not say them. It's no go, North thought. He can't say what he wants to say; he's afraid. They're all afraid; afraid of being laughed at; afraid of giving themselves away. . . . We're all afraid of each other, he thought; afraid of what? Of criticism; of laughter; or people who think differently. . . . That's what separates us; fear, he thought.

This is one of the major ideas of the novel: that people *can* know one another, but refuse to do so.

"I do not want to go back into my past, [Eleanor] was thinking. I want the present." This is another major idea: that the passage of time is anything but a tragedy; that human nature is in the process of becoming less imperfect, becoming in a creative evolution during which evil will be overcome and good triumph. This is the affirmation of the novel as a whole. Peggy mistakenly thinks that the past "was so interesting; so safe; so unreal—that past of the 'eighties; and to her, so beautiful in its unreality." But Eleanor, who has lived in that past, come through its goods and its bads, realizes that not the past but the future is safe and interesting, and that she must therefore live in the present. At the conclusion of the novel, during which Eleanor—somewhat like Bernard—has been moving toward a complete awareness, she has a final apprehension of meaning. Delia's party is breaking up; it is very late, almost dawn. Eleanor has been worrying about people's seeming inability to communicate: "She held her hands hollowed; she felt that she wanted to enclose the present moment; to make it stay; to fill it fuller and fuller, with the past the present and the future, until it shone, whole, bright, deep with understanding." At first she thinks this impossible.

> It's useless, she thought, opening her hands. It must drop. It must fall. And then? she thought. For her too there would be the endless night; the endless dark. She looked ahead of her as though she saw opening in front of her a very long dark tunnel. But, thinking of the dark, something baffled her; in fact it was growing light. The blinds were white.

Here, so far, is a situation exactly like that at the conclusion of *The Waves*. But *The Years* is not content to end here, with only an abstract statement; it goes on. The caretaker's two little children enter (Delia wishes to give them cake) and sing a song: "Etho passo tanno hai,/Fai donk to tu do," and so on. No one can understand a word of what they are singing: "It was so shrill, so discordant, so meaningless." But Eleanor, looking for a word that will describe this song—this strange, new language of the youngest generation—decides upon "beautiful." Then in the dawn Eleanor goes to the window. A cab stops in front of a house two doors down.

> She was watching the cab. A young man had got out; he paid the driver.
> Then a girl in a tweed travelling suit followed him. He fitted his latch-key to
> the door. "There," Eleanor murmured, as he opened the door and they
> stood for a moment on the threshold. "There!" she repeated as the door shut
> with a little thud behind them.
>   Then she turned round into the room. "And now?" she said
> . . . "And now?" she asked, holding out her hands to [Morris].

With an empathy like Clarissa's—an empathy that enabled her to "become" Martin in India—Eleanor looks at the newly married couple and grasps all the immense significance of their beginning: the pattern of a continual becoming toward right and good. She has been correct in her belief that "there must be another life. . . . Not in dreams; but here and now, in this room, with living people. . . . This is too short, too broken. We know nothing, even about ourselves. We're only just beginning . . . to understand, here and there." *The Years* concludes, just as *The Waves* had done, with a separate final descriptive sentence: "The sun had risen, and the sky above the houses wore an air of extraordinary beauty, simplicity and peace." This formalization of the philosophical perspective by means of immediate social and individual circumstance makes *The Years* the most persuasive of Virginia Woolf's novels. The final cab episode is additionally effective because it contrasts with a similar scene at the beginning of the novel when Delia, who wants very much to marry, watches from the same window a hansom approach the Pargiter house. And she wonders:

> Was it going to stop at their door or not? . . . to her regret, the cabman
> jerked his reins . . . the cab stopped two doors lower down . . . .
> they watched a young man . . . get out of the cab. He stretched up his hand
> to pay the driver. . . .
>   The young man ran up the steps into the house; the door shut upon him
> and the cab drove away. . . .
>   Dropping the blind, Delia turned, and coming back into the drawing-
> room, said suddenly:
>   "Oh, my God!"

Here is the idea of fulfillment and nonfulfillment; it appears very much as it had done in *The Waves*. Thus Eleanor, though she is a spinster, is fulfilled in her mental androgyny and empathy; on the other hand, Nicholas Pomjalovsky longs for a new world, and is constantly trying to make a speech in which he can articulate what he believes to be real. His inability to communicate, to surrender his identity, is symbolized—as was Neville's in *The Waves*—by his perversion. Sara Pargiter, perhaps

the most pathetic person in the novel, is another example of nonfulfillment, although she herself is not entirely to blame for her inability to
communicate. Extremely perceptive and sensitive, Sara is physically
deformed; her behavior becomes more and more erratic as she grows
older, her fantastic manner being a shield between herself and the society
that she feels hostile to her. She is reduced to poverty after her parents'
sudden death, and lives with her sister Maggie in a shabby walk-up flat.
Maggie—who resembles Susan of *The Waves*, though she is far more
human and successful a character—marries, and Sara is left alone. For a
time she turns to the Church of England; she finally falls in love, but with
Nicholas, who, although he loves her very much, is quite candid in
explaining why he cannot marry her. Sara's final rejection of society and
social intercourse is symbolized by her arriving at Delia's party—after a
dinner with North in her sordid boarding house, in what is perhaps the
most superbly achieved sequence in the novel—wearing one blue stocking and one white.

Although society is the immediate background of individual behavior in this novel, the use of society is not exactly conventional; it is not
one social code, a single set of manners, that is emphasized, but rather the
change from society to society—the social shift. As Virginia Woolf
wrote in *The Waves,* "Bodies, I note, already begin to look ordinary; but
what is behind them differs—the perspective." The very climax of the
novel is Eleanor's dismissal of the faithful (and wonderful) Pargiter
servant Crosby; together with Eleanor's sale of the Pargiter house, this
constitutes her disposal of the last remnants of the old culture and
tradition. This scene is filled with sadness and nostalgia; yet, although
Eleanor weeps, "she was so glad." After this it is Crosby who preserves
the old way, setting up pictures of the family in the little room where she
boards, until "it was quite like home." For Eleanor it is not the seeming
security of a traditional social context, but the apparently amorphous
becoming of the future, that has value. Static society, then—as distinct
from responsible human behavior—is repudiated in *The Years* too as a
superimposition. This is also made clear at Delia's final party, in a
"matter-spirit" contrast between Eleanor and her sister Milly. North
looks at Milly and her husband Hugh—both of whom exist entirely as
social creatures—and thinks, "Tut-tut-tut, and chew-chew-chew—as
they trod out the soft steamy straw in the stable; as they wallowed in the
primeval swamp, prolific, profuse, half-conscious." The damning word
is of course "half-conscious": Milly and Hugh have regressed until in
them, as in prehistoric life, awareness is choked with matter. For
Eleanor—and it is toward Eleanor's point of view that North is gradually
moving—life has not this static nature; it is "a perpetual discovery." She

perceives life intuitionally, and "intuition may be described as turning past and present into fact directly known by transforming it from mere matter into a creative process of duration."[6] The society, like the purely social being, is residual, "half-conscious." Eleanor, with an "unreasonable exaltation," feels in her seventies "that they were all young, with the future before them. Nothing was fixed; nothing was known; life was open and free before them." How completely this agrees with Bergson may be seen in his own statement: "Consciousness corresponds exactly to the living being's power of choice; it is coextensive with . . . possible action: consciousness is synonymous with invention and with freedom."[7] For just as matter is fixed, time—movement in becoming—is free. Eleanor fleetingly realizes this earlier in the novel; she leaves Maggie's home after an air raid, and looks up at the sky. "A broad fan of light, like the sail of a windmill, was sweeping slowly across the sky. It seemed to take what she was feeling and to express it broadly and simply, as if another voice were speaking in another language." This is significant, not only insofar as it underlines the function of the descriptive passages of the novel, but also when the unintelligible song of the children later recalls and emphasizes its meaning, shortly before Eleanor's own becoming brings her to complete awareness and the novel to an end. To think that the conclusion of *The Years* is "almost shocking in its irrelevance,"[8] or that the novel is "repetitious" and could have come to a close with the 1917 section just as well as with the 1937,[9] is probably to ignore or forget its meaning.

The Years has often been compared with other "period" novels of about the same time—*The Rainbow, The Old Wives' Tale,* and especially *The Forsyte Saga.* Of course *The Years* is much different from these novels,[10] and vastly superior to the last two of them. Galsworthy, however, is a few times interestingly akin to Virginia Woolf: although *The Forsyte Saga* presents human beings only as social specimens, whereas *The Years* traces Eleanor and the other Pargiters as developing individuals and as members of differing classes of a changing and developing society, nevertheless Galsworthy also toys with Bergsonistic

[6]Karin Stephen, *The Misuse of Mind: a Study of Bergson's Attack on Intellectualism* (New York: Harcourt, Brace, 1922), p. 102.

[7]Henri Bergson, *Creative Evolution,* trans. Arthur Mitchell (New York: Holt, 1911), pp. 263–264.

[8]Savage, loc. cit.

[9]David Daiches, "Virginia Woolf," in *The Novel and the Modern World* (Chicago: University of Chicago Press, 1939), p. 120.

[10]See, for example, Daiches, op. cit., pp. 111–112; Floris Delattre, 'La Durée bergsonienne dans le roman de Virginia Woolf," *Revue Anglo-Américaine* (December, 1931), pp. 289ff.

concepts; in the "Indian Summer of a Forsyte," for example, Old Jolyon thinks of a "Life-Force."[11] But the differences between his reaction to Bergsonism and Virginia Woolf's (or Joyce's or Lawrence's) are obvious; his is a blind and fateful force, making free will impossible and people therefore irresponsible. Galsworthy's life force is antithetical to Virginia Woolf's; perhaps halfway between the two is Bernard Shaw's version, as it can be seen in such plays as *Man and Superman,* or *Heartbreak House,* or *Back to Methuselah.* For Shaw, "to be in hell is to drift: to be in heaven is to steer."[12]

Both in philosophical perspective and in social consciousness, however, *The Years* is most significantly comparable to Proust's novel. Perhaps more than any other of Virginia Woolf's novels, *The Years* both resembles and differs from *À la Recherche du temps perdu.* Both novels begin with the security of a traditional family culture, move through the First World War, and conclude with a long party scene, having traced the development of many individual characters and the transition of a society. The final section of *The Years,* indeed, is especially similar to the great party in *Le Temps retrouvé*, not only in its general proportion and significance, but in several individual details. The hypocritical upstart Mme Verdurin has finally realized her greatest dream—she, of the noble forehead and hypersensitive emotions, is Princesse de Guermantes. The framework of Proust's party, then, is very like that of Virginia Woolf's, although it is not Delia's character but her house that achieves the effect. Again there are the same painful contrasts between youth grown old and new, unknown youth; since North has been in Africa and just returned to London, the impact of the change affects him just as it affects Marcel, returned to society after his long illness. And of course there are the perceptions of reality, Marcel's before the party and Eleanor's after the party.

In *The Years,* however, no such "résurrection de la mémoire" exists as can be found in *Le Temps retrouvé* and in Virginia Woolf's own earlier novels. The whole past is not explicitly charged into the present moment as it was, for example, in *Orlando.* Eleanor, watching the newly married couple, does recapture and hold time past in time present, but this is accomplished implicitly and not given the emphasis or role it had received in the earlier books. To be sure, the present moment does shine "whole, bright, deep with understanding," and is filled "with the past the present and the future"; but it is the future—and not the past—that Eleanor realizes most emphatically. Furthermore, although she knows

[11] John Galsworthy, *The Forsyte Saga* (New York: Scribner's, 1934), pp. 59, 61.

[12] Bernard Shaw, *Man and Superman,* in *Selected Plays,* III (New York: Dodd, Mead, 1948), p. 646.

now that she will not disappear into "the endless night; the endless dark," it is not the sense of her own immortality that most impresses and satisfies her, but rather the sense that life is improvable as well as everlasting, that good can triumph over and annihilate evil. *The Years* is not a triumph of consciousness over the past so much as it is a consciousness of triumph in the future. *To the Lighthouse* concludes when Lily Briscoe, exhausted but triumphant, says, "I have had my vision" and puts aside her paintbrush. *The Years,* on the other hand, concludes with Eleanor reaching out, asking, " 'And now?' " The present moment is no longer simply an end in itself; it is at once an end and a means. *The Years* therefore overcomes what is a fairly serious limitation in Virginia Woolf's earlier novels.

This new emphasis follows quite logically from the stuff of which *The Years* is made. Eleanor as one individual realizes the present moment—perceives completely the nature of reality—as an end in itself: she has grasped the total meaning of her own life. But Eleanor as a member of society, the public as distinct from the private Eleanor, must perceive her knowledge as means rather than end. To do otherwise would be, in this case, to revert as social being to the dead Victorian culture; society cannot be conceived of as recapturing its past history, but only as using awareness of the past as a standard for future progress. The private Eleanor can say that she has had her vision; the public Eleanor, recognizing that vision as a means, must ask, " 'And now?' " As one human being, Eleanor responds; as a member of society, she must *behave* in the light of her response. "Society" and "behavior" are, in this sense, far more profound than the behavior of Milly and Hugh in the society of Delia's party. In that society, indeed, faced with that behavior, Eleanor loses her consciousness: while Milly prattles, Eleanor falls asleep:

> Eleanor snored. She was nodding off, shamelessly, helplessly. There was an obscenity in unconsciousness, [North] thought. Her mouth was open; her head was on one side.
>
> But now it was his turn. Silence gaped. One has to egg it on, he thought; somebody has to say something, or human society would cease. Hugh would cease; Milly would cease.

If this society is matter, and Eleanor's consciousness spirit, then her final awareness is Eleanor's individual victory over precisely this materiality, and her perception of a future victory for consciousness itself. Here Eleanor is defending herself from matter by falling asleep; when she wakens, she remembers her sleep as "a gap—a gap filled with the golden light of lolling candles"; this is of course the old image for spirit, the flame-candle dichotomy of "Kew Gardens." Society—real society—is not the static code of manners, but the becoming reflected in the very transition from one code to another. Value is becoming; becoming is value.

Virginia Woolf was again to employ this new emphasis upon the collective future rather than the individual past in *Between the Acts. The Years*, because of this concept of a becoming society as well as becoming individual beings, has a scope and range not to be found in any of the earlier novels; and it makes an affirmation about human life and experience more persuasive than that made by *The Waves,* where the collective becoming of Bernard's final challenge was expressed upon a purely symbolic level. Here the entire perspective has been explored, the entire significance discovered: the variegated spectacle focused by the glass roof is colored with sharp sunlight; the glass roof itself is both spectacle and sun.

Many critics have considered *The Years* a complete failure;[13] E. M. Forster was expressing a popular attitude toward this novel when he said that it was, like *Night and Day,* an "experiment in the realistic tradition . . . . as in *Night and Day,* she deserts poetry, and again she fails."[14] On the contrary, *The Years* seems to me to be Virginia Woolf's best novel; it follows consistently the essential pattern of thought seen in her earlier novels, but extends both philosophical and formal perspective further than any of them; it flawlessly formalizes a more comprehensive idea of "life itself," and it does this not by deserting what Forster calls "poetry," but by transforming and assimilating public with private values into a harmonious whole, in accordance with Virginia Woolf's vision of experience, yet justifiable outside the boundaries of that vision as it appeared in the earlier books. If by "poetry" Forster means prose style rather than exclusive symbolism, again *The Years* is considerably superior to *The Waves,* in which the "elevated style" so often becomes overemotional and gets in its own way, especially when the reader remembers that it was written by so fine a stylist as Virginia Woolf. Read hastily, *The Years* might seem no more than a "conventional novel," beautifully written—although much of it would certainly be puzzling—whereas, read carefully, it shows itself a work in which Virginia Woolf used all her treasure of technical ability to make of conventional novel form something at once traditional and new.

[13]Sympathetic as well as adverse critics hold this opinion; see for example, Deborah Newton, *Virginia Woolf* (Melbourne: University of Melbourne Press, 1946), pp. 54–55; R. Chambers, *The Novels of Virginia Woolf* (Edinburgh: Oliver and Boyd, 1947), p. 46.

[14]E. M. Forster, *Virginia Woolf* (Rede Lecture, May 29, 1941) (Cambridge: University Press, 1942), p. 17.

Werner J. Deiman

History, Pattern, and Continuity
in Virginia Woolf

> *A people without history*
> *Is not redeemed from time, for history is a pattern*
> *Of timeless moments. So, while the light fails*
> *On a winter's afternoon, in a secluded chapel*
> *History is now and England.*
> —T. S. Eliot, "Little Gidding," *Four Quartets*

From the beginning of her career through the last year of her life a profound historical sense and perspective informed Virginia Woolf's thought and development. Significantly, as late as September 12, 1940, her *Diary* records how she "conceived, or re-moulded, an idea for a Common History book—to read from one end of literature including biography; and range at will, consecutively,"[1] and three months before her death, during the Blitz over Britain, her imagination juxtaposed the burning of London, including the destruction of eight city churches and

---

[1] Virginia Woolf, *A Writer's Diary*, Leonard Woolf (ed.) (New York: Harcourt Brace Jovanovich, 1953), p. 335; further references will be preceded by *D*. Other Woolf works cited in this essay, with their respective abbreviations, are as follows: *V—The Voyage Out* (London: Hogarth Press, 1957); *N—Night and Day* (London: Hogarth Press, 1960); *J—Jacob's Room* (London: Hogarth Press, 1960); *M—Mrs. Dalloway* (New York: Harcourt Brace Jovanovich, 1925); *R—A Room of One's Own* (London: Hogarth Press, 1959);

Werner J. Deiman, "History, Pattern, and Continuity in Virginia Woolf," Contemporary Literature, *vol. XV, no. 1 (Winter, 1974) pp. 49–66. Reprinted by permission of the author and the University of Wisconsin Press.*

the Guildhall, with the "Great Fire" of London, which she had been
reading about a few nights before "in a very accurate detailed book" (*D*,
January 1, 1941, p. 348). Although Woolf's achievement is correctly
linked with the novel-of-manners tradition and identified with technical
innovations, aestheticism, the problems of identity, visionary themes,
and mysticism, it is also clear that a very conscious and constant awareness of the historical past not only was part of her daily living present but
also helped shape and structure the very essence of her evolution and
thought. A careful reading of *Between the Acts* and the last two years of
the *Diary* will disclose the extent to which history is the predominant
subject of both that posthumous novel and Woolf's most private and
agonized thoughts. While her native temperament and the England which
she loved induced historical considerations, and while she realized, like
Santayana, that those who would not learn from the past would be forced
to repeat it, the rapidly accelerating developments of the War coupled
with Woolf's own psychological crisis intensified that much more her
quest for a belief in history as pattern and continuity. In short, the
existential questions of human life pressed upon her at the end in one final
and absolute confrontation.

Historical perspectives begin appearing, however, much earlier in
Virginia Woolf's life and career than most commentators have sufficiently emphasized. The *Diary* reveals how her fascination with history
and historical change was an early one: "It was the Elizabethan prose
writers I loved first and most wildly, stirred by Hakluyt. . . . I used to
. . . dream of those obscure adventurers. . . . I was then writing a
long picturesque essay upon the Christian religion . . . proving that
man has need of a God; but the God was described in process of change;
and I also wrote a history of Women; and a history of my own family
. . ." (*D*, December 8, 1929, p. 147).

The two early and basically nonexperimental novels, *The Voyage
Out* and *Night and Day,* include the theme of history and demonstrate a
sensitivity to the process of change. The former reveals again her delight
in the Elizabethans and in projecting oneself into their world: "Since the
time of Elizabeth very few people had seen the river, and nothing had
been done to change its appearance from what it was to the eyes of the

DM—*The Death of the Moth and Other Essays* (Baltimore: Penguin Books, 1961); *W*—*The
Waves* (New York: Harcourt Brace Jovanovich, 1931); *Y*—*The Years* (London: Hogarth
Press, 1958); *L*—*To the Lighthouse* (New York: Harcourt Brace Jovanovich, 1927);
B—*Between the Acts* (New York: Harcourt Brace Jovanovich, 1941). All excerpts from the
works of Virginia Woolf are reprinted by permission of Harcourt Brace Jovanovich, Inc.

The epigraph is taken from T. S. Eliot, *Complete Poems and Plays* (New York: Harcourt
Brace Jovanovich, 1952), pp. 144–145.

Elizabethan voyagers. The time of Elizabeth was only distant from the present time by a moment of space compared with the ages which had passed . . ." (*V*, p. 323). Reminiscent of Bergson, the past is depicted as not only contained in the present but also identified with it as virtually one and the same. In *Night and Day,* accepting the process of change becomes the ultimate wisdom which Katherine can acquire, and her dearly won perspective takes precedence over any considerations of the goal to be reached: "It's life that matters, nothing but life—the process of discovering, the everlasting and perpetual process . . . not the discovery itself at all" (*N*, p. 138). The wisdom of Katherine's discovery is one example of the extent to which the nineteenth century was so much a part of Woolf's legacy and a major influence on her development. In Goethe's *Faust,* for example, the hero's redemption is granted on the basis of his commitment to striving and discovery, and in Dostoevsky's *Notes from Underground,* another work with which she was familiar, we read: "And who knows . . . perhaps the only goal on earth to which mankind is striving lies in this incessant process of attaining, in other words, in life itself, and not in the thing to be attained. . . .''[2] Still an earlier affirmation of process and becoming is to be seen in Montaigne who both provided Woolf with the subject of an essay and also furnished Leonard Woolf with the title for the last volume of his autobiography: "The journey not the arrival matters."

Jacob's Room includes many details about ruins of Roman civilization and reflects the frequent traces of the Roman legacy (especially in Sussex) which fascinated Virginia Woolf. The book describes its hero playing in a Roman fortress and his mother sitting on the raised circle of the Roman camp, while the Rev. Jaspar Floyd has dug up "Cannon-balls; arrow heads; Roman glass and a forceps green with verdigris . . . in the Roman camp on Dods Hill . . ." (*J*, p. 17). The vision, in *Night and Day*, of ceaseless change and the perspective which dictates an acceptance of the same becomes, in *Jacob's Room* and the succeeding novels, a more profound and personal commitment to one's sense of inheritance and the obligations involved in seeing oneself as both heir and eventual benefactor. At Cambridge Jacob hears the clock, which conveys to him "a sense of old buildings and time; and himself the inheritor; and then tomorrow . . ." (*J*, p. 43). Later he admires the beauty of the Cornish hills, discovers an inextricable relationship between the beautiful and the sad, tries to analyze his sorrow, and finally frames it with an historical perspective: "It is brewed by the earth itself. It comes from the houses on the coast. We start transparent, and then the cloud thickens. All history

[2]Fyodor Dostoevsky, *Notes from Underground,* in *The Continental Edition of World Masterpieces,* ed. Maynard Mack (New York: W. W. Norton, 1962), p. 1541.

backs our pane of glass. To escape is vain" (*J*, p. 47). In the same novel
as the author's eye moves over the Thames and St. Paul's to an old man,
who takes on symbolic dimensions, the focus of Woolf's thoughts again
becomes historical as she raises the questions: "But what century have
we reached? Has this procession from the Surrey side to the Strand gone
on for ever? That old man has been crossing the Bridge these six hundred
years. . . . No one stands still. It seems as if we marched to the sound of
music . . . perhaps these same drums and trumpets—the ecstasy and
hubbub of the soul" (*J*, p. 112). Time is depicted here as a relentlessly
flowing continuum which brings the past into the future but also,
paradoxically, as the agent of a kind of constancy. The author does not
identify the old man as one of many who have crossed the Bridge but
specifies that he alone, emblematic of humanity, has done so, and for
some six hundred years. By implication we are reminded that generations
of the future will continue to see this very same man.

In *Mrs. Dalloway* not only does the author's voice bring together the
two seemingly disparate personalities and spatial worlds of the heroine
and Septimus Smith; she also impregnates the present moment of consciousness with a sense of the historical past which, in turn, projects itself
forward into the future. Early in the novel we recall the incident of the
mysterious motor car with its passenger of national stature. The immediacy of the present moment, with all of its charismatic allure centered as it
is amidst the pomp and majesty of London, is juxtaposed to the remotest
future, when the secret passenger will be known and, at the same time,
London will have become the ruins appropriate for an archeological dig:
"which will be known to curious antiquaries, sifting the ruins of time,
when London is a grass-grown path and all those hurrying along the
pavement this Wednesday morning are but bones with a few wedding
rings mixed up in their dust and the gold stoppings of innumerable
decayed teeth. The face in the motor car will then be known" (*M*, p. 23).
A figure comparable to the old man crossing the bridge in *Jacob's Room*
appears during one of Peter Walsh's walks, when he hears an elderly
woman singing who suddenly takes on visionary significance as his
thoughts extend all the way back to the beginning of time and forward
into an infinite future; the passage must be quoted at length:

> Through all ages—when the pavement was grass, when it was swamp,
> through the age of tusk and mammoth, through the age of silent sunrise,
> the battered woman . . . stood singing of love—love which has lasted a
> million years, she sang, love which prevails, and millions of years ago,
> her lover, who had been dead these centuries, had walked, she crooned,
> with her in May; but in the course of ages, long as summer days . . . he
> had gone; death's enormous sickle had swept those tremendous hills, and

when at last she laid her hoary and immensely aged head on the earth, now become a mere cinder of ice, she implored the Gods to lay by her side a bunch of purple heather, there on her high burial place which the last rays of the last sun caressed; for then the pageant of the universe would be over (*M*, pp. 122–23).

Life is depicted as a pageant in which the time span of epochs, centuries, millions of years, or summer days is entirely relative. Both the elderly man of *Jacob's Room* and this woman become in a very real way the embodiment of history. They are drawn with precise strokes and details, reflective of the author's obsession with the uniqueness of each human identity, but they are also nameless and evoke our sense of the symbolic quality of their depiction, of history in the flesh, our overwhelming intuition of historical continuity amidst change and flux.

When we become privy to the thoughts of Rezia, Septimus' Italian-born and long-suffering wife, we see her in Regent's Park and read how "at midnight, when all boundaries are lost, the country reverts to its ancient shape, as the Romans saw it, lying cloudy, when they landed, and the hills had no names and rivers wound they knew not where . . ." (*M*, p. 35). The passage implies the author's identification of Rezia with both her Roman forebears and the pristine, somewhat bewildered quality of their response to new terrain and geography as she, their remote descendant, makes her way in the same foreign country, beset by the hallucinations of a husband who has become a stranger to her. We find a remarkably similar passage in the *Diary* as the historical past suddenly merges with the present moment of Virginia Woolf's consciousness: "Sitting by the road under the Roman wall. . . . Reason why the hills are still Roman—the landscape immortal . . . what they saw I see. The wind, the June wind, the water, and snow. Sheep bedded in the long turf like pearls. No shade, no shelter. Romans looking over the border. Now nothing comes" (*D*, June 16, 1938, pp. 285–286). Just as Virginia Woolf's thoughts and her description of Rezia's present condition recall the Roman past, so does Richard Dalloway, as he passes Buckingham Palace and the memorial to Queen Victoria, feel both his identity and pride linked to his English heritage: "he liked being ruled by the descendant of Horsa; he liked continuity; and the sense of handing on the traditions of the past" (*M*, p. 177).

Three works published between 1929 and 1932 develop further the author's preoccupation with historical perspective and the themes of continuity and the inheritor. *A Room of One's Own* articulates Virginia Woolf's reverence for the continuity of civilization, the sense, which she shared with her close friend T. S. Eliot, of a distinct tradition which has

been inherited, is evolving, and in which the individual authorial voice
resonates with clear overtones of the past:

> Without those forerunners, Jane Austen and the Brontës and George Eliot
> could no more have written than Shakespeare could have written without
> Marlowe, or Marlowe without Chaucer, or Chaucer without those forgotten
> poets who paved the ways and tamed the natural savagery of the tongue. For
> masterpieces are not single and solitary births; they are the outcome of many
> years of thinking in common, of thinking by the body of the people, so that
> the experience of the mass is behind the single voice (*R*, p. 98).

Three years later, in "A Letter to a Young Poet," thoughts of a similar
vein were shared with the Woolfs' friend, employee, and later partner,
John Lehmann. Here she specified that he was "a poet in whom live all
the poets of the past, from whom all poets in time to come will spring.
You have a touch of Chaucer in you, and something of Shakespeare;
Dryden, Pope, Tennyson . . . stir in your blood. . . . In short you are
an immensely ancient, complex, and continuous character . . ."
(*DM*, p. 181). In *The Waves*, published in 1931, Louis hears Dr. Crane
read the lesson from a Bible and thinks how "I recover my continuity,
as he reads" (*W*, p. 35). Later he imagines himself "the friend of
Richelieu, or the Duke of St. Simon" (*W*, p. 52). Cherishing his associations with his friends, he comments that "Above all, we have inherited traditions" and exclaims, "Blessings be on all traditions . . ."
(*W*, p. 58). When he forces himself "to state, if only in one line of
unwritten poetry, this moment; to mark this inch in the long, long
history that began in Egypt, in the time of the Pharaohs, when women
carried red pitchers to the Nile" (*W*, p. 66), he finally identifies himself
with that past as he finds "relics of myself in the sand that women
made thousands of years ago, when I heard songs by the Nile . . ." (*W*,
p. 127). In a similar way the sense of time and the scope of history
dominate Bernard's anguished thoughts later in the novel as he thinks to
himself: "Our English past—one inch of light" and as he tries "to
recover, as we walk, the sense of time . . ." (*W*, p. 227). Recalling the
dinner which he and his friends had all enjoyed at Hampton Court Palace,
with all of its historical richness, and a favorite place of the author and her
Bloomsbury friends, he thinks: "The wind, the rush of wheels became
the roar of time, and we rushed—where? And who were we? We were
extinguished for a moment, went out like sparks in burnt paper and the
blackness roared. Past time, past history we went" (*W*, p. 277).

Bernard's depiction of the moment in flight, used to convey his
suffering, is paralleled by the author's entry in her *Diary* in 1929 at the
height of her work on *The Waves:*

> Now is life very solid or very shifting? I am haunted by the two
> contradictions. This has gone on for ever; will last for ever; goes down to
> the bottom of the world—this moment I stand on. Also it is transitory,
> flying, diaphanous. I shall pass like a cloud on the waves. Perhaps it may
> be that though we change, one flying after another, so quick, so quick, yet
> we are somehow successive and continuous we human beings . . . (*D*,
> January 4, 1929, p. 138).

What we see in the essay, letter, novel, and diary are, on the one hand,
the overwhelming sense of the absolute and ultimate importance of the
individual, conditioned as he is by the transitory moment, a fact which
results in inevitable personal anguish, and, on the other, the author's
resolution, in her profoundest moments, of this suffering through the
long view of historical perspective and continuity. In short, the individual and his moment are, on the ultimate level, transcended by a vision
of the human race, its evolution, and history.

In *The Years* the final scene describes the passing of a long night
which corresponds to the mood of the major character, Eleanor. As she
tries desperately to believe that there is another life and acknowledges
that she and her friends are only beginning to know anything about
themselves, she holds her hands hollowed and wants ''to enclose the
present moment; to make it stay; to fill it fuller and fuller, with the past,
the present and the future, until it shone, whole, bright, deep with
understanding'' (*Y*, p. 462). Here again, it is significant that only the past
and the future can lend understanding to the present. Overcome by
dejection she opens her hands and concludes that only an endless night,
''a very long dark tunnel,'' is her lot and is suddenly startled to realize
that a new day is dawning, as the final sentence of the novel reads: ''The
sun had risen, and the sky above the houses wore an air of extraordinary
beauty, simplicity, and peace'' (*Y*, p. 469). The metaphorical significance of the light emphasizes the importance of the present as a period of
transition leading towards something else—especially, the understanding which comes from hindsight. Eleanor's vision of time becoming
represents, in short, a successful turn from Peggy's lamentation earlier in
the novel over ''Death; or worse—tyranny; brutality; torture; the fall of
civilisation; the end of freedom'' (*Y*, p. 418).

In *Between the Acts* Virginia Woolf was to confront one final time
the imminent possibility of death and torture (for which petrol was kept in
the garage for suicide in the event that the Germans conquered), and
while the novel was in progress she and her husband listened and read
each day of death and brutality and witnessed the disastrous events taking
place on the Continent. The tragic intensity and desperation of the times
forced her to an almost obsessive preoccupation with history on virtually

every page of this posthumous novel. While the plethora of historical details is beyond recording *in toto* in an article, it is necessary to cite some of them.

The age of tusk and mammoth mentioned in *Mrs. Dalloway*[3] reappears in this later novel, now expanded to include the iguanodon and mastodon. These are among the many extinct creatures which fascinate Mrs. Swithin so much in her *Outline of History,* part of which, in turn, describes prehistoric England joined to the Continent. We read of "her imaginative reconstruction of the past" (*B*, p. 9), and of how "she was given to increasing the bounds of the moment by flights into past or future," a statement which recalls Woolf's brief mention in the *Diary* for 1932 of how "the downs this windy sunny day looked wild and remote; and I could rethink them into uncultivated land again" (*D*, August 5, p. 179). Mrs. Swithin has been told by her dentist that savages could perform operations on the brain and that they had false teeth which, in turn, had been invented in the time of the pharaohs. The Swithin ancestry, unlike the Olivers', goes back to before the Conquest, and the delivery boy's name, like those of his customers, is in the Domesday Book. The house Pointz Hall itself has evolved in history, having had, before the Reformation, a chapel which had later become a larder. The description of the land on which it stands, as found in "Figgis's Guide Book" of 1833, corresponds to the present scene in 1939. The Barn had been built over 700 years ago and reminds various people of either Greek temples, the middle ages, or some other earlier period, but "scarcely anybody of the present moment . . ." (*B*, p. 99). The historical consciousness of this work extends to the specification, previously rare, of particular years in earlier centuries, such as 1833, mentioned above, or William Dodge's guess that a coffee cup dates from 1760, or the fact that the man in the painting in the dining room was buried around 1750. In the audience at the pageant, the mysterious "great lady in the bath chair" recalls the elderly man in *Jacob's Room* and the streetsinger in *Mrs. Dalloway* and suggests the living essence or archetype of primeval man before he even evolved into man: "so indigenous was she that even her body, crippled by arthritis, resembled an uncouth, nocturnal animal, now nearly extinct . . ." (*B*, pp. 93–94).

But even more important than the historical consciousness is the related theme of continuity—the continuity of history in which change and evolution take place. In the beginning of the novel little George

---

[3]In *To the Lighthouse* there is a brief mention of "a mammoth [which] had been dug up in a London Street" (p. 281), but otherwise the theme of history or evolution is conspicuously absent from this novel.

admires the flower and can see that "the tree was beyond the flower; the grass, the flower and the tree were entire" (*B*, p. 11). His perception of continuity parallels Yeats's query in "Among School Children": "O chestnut-tree, great-rooted blossomer, / Are you the leaf, the blossom or the bole?"[4] and corresponds to the sense of continuity associated with Mrs. Swithin, who has been nailing the placard on the barn for years and whose words mentioning the annual ritual are compared to the peal of a chime of bells, with one sound inevitably coming after another. Her brother Bart also perceives a continuum in the labors of the Rev. Streatfield, who was "perpetually repairing the perpetually falling steeple" (*B*, p. 25). Of George's mother, Isa, we learn how "Every summer, for seven summers now, Isa had heard the same words. . . . The same chime followed the same chime" (*B*, p. 22), but this year, after the church bells stop, she thinks: "There was not going to be another note" (*B*, p. 207). Her ominous intuition of finality is paralleled by Mrs. Swithin's realization that so much of the beauty of the view from Pointz Hall derives from one's awareness that "It'll be there . . . when we're not" (*B*, p. 53). Mrs. Swithin's emphasis on the earth and Nature, which survive man's mortality, is repeated later when she shows William Dodge the library and runs her hands over some books in the wall on the landing. Her thoughts are momentarily pulled backward but enunciate nonetheless the theme of continuity and tradition as she tells him, "Here are the poets from whom we descend by way of the mind . . ." (*B*, p. 68). Her statement emphasizes a nobler, grander sense of heritage than blood lineage and echoes what we have already read in "A Letter to a Young Poet" and *A Room of One's Own*.

Lucy and Bart's consciousness of old age and inevitable death, Isa's awareness of crisis in her marriage, plus the reminders of war and death both overhead and across the Channel—all of these factors comprise a paradox for, at one and the same time, they point to a no-exit conclusion in the form of death, possible divorce, and war, and also intensify that much more the mind's need to sense continuity, to remember what does survive, to perceive the perpetual, the series, the repetition of ritual, the constant inevitability of both challenge and response. What is finally so moving about *Between the Acts* is its desperate vision and need to *get beyond* the crisis of the immediate present, to *believe* that this present moment is not the end, is not to be understood by itself but is rather another period of transition from the past and leading to something else. Ernst Cassirer's comment in *An Essay on Man* is à propos: "Organic life exists only insofar as it evolves in time. . . . We cannot describe the

[4]W. B. Yeats, *Collected Poems* (New York: Macmillan, 1959), p. 214.

momentary state of an organism without taking its history into consideration and without referring it to a future state for which this state is merely a point of passage."[5]

The pageant, of course, becomes the major vehicle in *Between the Acts* for its vision of continuity and constitutes a kind of history of England such as Virginia Woolf had depicted earlier, with deliberate caprice, in *Orlando*. We have already seen Woolf's depiction of life as a kind of pageant in *Mrs. Dalloway,* where the elderly woman singing inspires a vision of "the last rays of the last sun," when "the pageant of the universe would be over," and in *The Waves* Bernard delights "to find the pageant of existence roaring, in a theatre for instance" (*W,* p. 270). Here a real pageant is used to embody some of her love for and debt to those writers from whom she felt descended by way of the mind. It comprises a brilliantly inventive, sometimes satirical valentine to literary history, a tradition which she loved and in which the *Diary* reveals she hoped she herself would be immortalized. In the last year of her life, very little was certain in Virginia Woolf's consciousness, and the *Diary* became a desperate substitute for the audience which could no longer be counted on:

> It struck me that one curious feeling is, that the writing "I" has vanished. No audience. No echo. That's part of one's death. . . . No echo comes back. . . . Those familiar circumvolutions—those standards—which have for so many years given back an echo and so thickened my identity are all wide and wild as the desert now (*D*, June 9, 22, 1940, pp. 323, 325).

A plethora of literary allusions is to be found in and between the acts of the pageant which, like history, seems basically so fragmented and can be given continuity only in the vision of its artist-creator. The audience's attempts to understand and recognize, indeed, to see, are to be equated with man's attempts to glean understanding from the cavalcade of historical events. The absurdities and accidents involved in the production are no greater than those of history itself. The obsessive and even mystical preoccupation with time, which characterizes all of Woolf's writing, has been brilliantly encapsulated in one final *tour de force* which, in a real sense, transcends time itself and extends Bernard's mediation in *The Waves:* "But we . . . for one moment out of what measureless abundance of past time and time to come, burnt there triumphant. The moment was all; the moment was enough" (*W,* p. 278). Here, the individual moment, however exquisite, is not sufficient unto itself in the author's vision. The exhaustion and pain of old age, the innocence and ecstasy of youth, and the confusion and tensions

[5]Ernst Cassirer, *An Essay on Man* (New York: Doubleday, 1953), p. 72.

of middle age are all overshadowed by the clouds of war which, at one and the same time, rob the moment of perfection and serenity and yet lend a peculiar richness and intensity of beauty reminiscent of Keats and Pater. England and the life which the author loved are threatened—as well as the kind of civilization and climate which could afford the savoring of "the moment." As her friend E. M. Forster put it: "She loved her country— her country that is 'country,' and emerges from the unfathomable past. She takes us back in this exquisite final tribute, and she points us on, and she shows us . . . something more solid than patriotic history, and something better worth dying for."[6]

The author's lifelong preoccupation with the spaces between sounds, words, and actions is reflected in the pageant, which concentrates on relatively simple, trivial situations and persons rather than major movements and so-called makers of history; like the rest of the novel it is oriented towards what happened or what life was like in different periods of English history *between* the major acts of central figures. These lesser citizens and happenings are of no small importance or diminished interest. In a sense Woolf was fulfilling in this final opus a wish which she had expressed sixteen years before, in the *Diary* for 1925, where we read: "I want to read voraciously and gather material for the *Lives of the Obscure*—which is to tell the whole history of England in one obscure life after another" (*D*, July 20, p. 79). Two years later she mentioned how she had "a plan already to get historical manuscripts and write . . ." (*D*, February 28, 1927, p. 103) this same work, of which a few biographical essays have come down to us.

The reporter's description of the pageant restates the theme of continuity as he notes: "Miss La Trobe conveyed to the audience Civilization (the wall) in ruins; rebuilt . . . by human effort . . ." (*B*, p. 181). And the Rev. G. W. Streatfield later explicates the pageant to his audience, his remarks emphasizing especially the continuity of human perseverance: "We were shown, unless I mistake, the effort renewed" (*B*, pp. 191–192).

At the end of the pageant we hear music and, for the last time, Virginia Woolf emphasizes the continuum of life, history, and civilization which, in turn, unites the whole of man in one total identity and effort and brings together the one and the many:

> Like quicksilver sliding, filings magnetized, the distracted united. The tune began; the first note meant a second; the second a third. Then down beneath a force was born in opposition; then another. On different levels they diverged. On different levels ourselves went forward; flower gathering some on the surface; others descending to wrestle with the meaning; but all

[6]E. M. Forster, *Virginia Woolf* (New York: Harcourt Brace Jovanovich, 1942), p. 18.

comprehending; all enlisted. The whole population of the mind's immeasurable profundity came flocking; from the unprotected, the unskinned; and dawn rose; and azure; from chaos and cacophony measure; but not the melody of surface sound alone controlled it; but also the warring battle-plumed warriors straining asunder: To part? No. Compelled from the ends of the horizon; recalled from the edge of appalling crevasses; they crashed; solved; united (*B*, p. 189).

The verbalized transcription of the music comprises perhaps the single most impressive passage of the book and articulates the author's most profound and all-inclusive vision of an historical perspective. It is at once both literal and metaphorical. We see the recurrent theme of series and continuity, with one note following another and all falling into a meaningful pattern which, in turn, includes the inevitable counterpoint of forces born in opposition but nonetheless resolved. The Hegelian overtones are obvious. As we have seen at the very end of *The Years*, here a new dawn emerges from darkness and chaos. The musical melody includes not only "surface sound" or pure harmony but also the crash and dissonance of "the warring battle-plumed warriors straining asunder." From disparity and conflict finally issue solution, unity, and pattern. Significantly, during the height of her work on *Between the Acts* the *Diary* reveals that Virginia Woolf was reading "Ruth Benedict with pressure of suggestions—about culture patterns . . ." (*D*, July 26, 1940, p. 327); presumably the book was *Patterns of Culture*.

Except for *Orlando,* whose capricious tone and fanciful design place it beyond the scope of this essay, no other book of Virginia Woolf addresses itself so passionately and particularly to the facts of change or indicates the extent to which the author's vision, however basically aristocratic and rooted in tradition, could welcome and embrace an inevitable phenomenon, history in the making, especially in the light of a philosophical perspective. A minor character, Mrs. Lynn Jones, thinks to herself: "Change had to come . . . or there'd have been yards and yards of Papa's beard, of Mama's knitting. Nowadays her son-in-law was clean shaven. Her daughter had a refrigerator. . . . Change had to come, unless things were perfect; in which case she supposed they resisted Time. Heaven was changeless" (*B*, p. 174). As she looks to the martins later her vision connects a continuity of change with the condition of unity and fulfillment; the birds "seemed to foretell what after all the *Times* was saying yesterday. Homes will be built. Each flat with its refrigerator, in the crannied wall. Each of us a free man; plates washed by machinery; not an aeroplane to vex us; all liberated; made whole . . ." (*B*, pp. 182–183).

Much of *Between the Acts* thus concerns the problems of society, social change, and personal behavior, as seen against an historical perspective. We are told that some "snobs" who are working on the pageant "have taken indelibly the print of some three hundred years of customary behaviour" (*B*, p. 27). When the elder Mr. Oliver meets Mrs. Manresa, he "bowed deep" over her hand, while "a century ago, he would have kissed it" (*B*, p. 38). At the end of the novel he thinks, as he watches the actors: "He must respect the conventions. So he stopped, by the pool" (*B*, p. 203); of the rest of the audience we read how "They kept their distance from the dressing room; they respected the conventions" (*B*, p. 151) and hear their hypocritical comment on the " 'delicious tea!' . . . disgusting though it was, like rust boiled in water, and the cake fly-blown. But they had a duty to society" (*B*, p. 103). While Virginia Woolf revered so much of the past, her respect was directed to specific individuals and ways of thinking and living and nothing was more meaningless to her than mere lip service to idols or norms which had simply been passed on by history. And so, in contrast to the old and landed Anglo-Saxon families, we encounter such exotic newcomers as the Manresas (Ralph Manresa is specified as a Jew) who not only enjoy driving elegant cars with their initials on the door but who are also "bringing the old houses up to date, adding bathrooms" (*B*, p. 74). His wife, the exotic Mrs. Manresa, represents a kind of unabashed, however amusing, sexuality, but she is also specified, some seven times, as a symbolic "wild child of nature" (*B*, pp. 41, 44, 50, 55, 79, 102, 177) and the author's tone in equating her with "fresh air that blew in" (*B*, p. 41) is unmistakably positive. As an invigorating, vital force, she is in sharp contrast to the artificiality and stuffiness of manner so common among many in the audience and it is significant that Giles Oliver, whose conformity to the convention of blazer and flannels is automatic and, therefore, in the author's view, hollow, is strongly attracted to her.

Like the socially liberated Mrs. Manresa, the producer of the pageant, Miss La Trobe, is, in addition, artistically freed and therefore fated to suffer that much more conflict with her society. About her plans for the pageant we read: "Expenses had to be kept down. Ten pounds was the limit. Thus conventions were outraged. Swathed in conventions, they couldn't see, as she could, that a dish cloth wound round a head in the open looked much richer than real silk" (*B,* p. 64). As an artist and lesbian Virginia Woolf's equivalent of Philoctetes is specified as a social outcast who will be snubbed by Mrs. Chalmers and the other women in the cottages and is also someone whom, we are told, "Nature had somehow set . . . apart from her kind" (*B*, p. 211), but who is also regarded, significantly, by Mrs. Swithin as "a lady of wonderful energy'' (*B*, p. 58). She, Mrs. Manresa, and William Dodge are, like the aristocratic Bloomsbury bohemian herself, Virginia Woolf, genuinely independent, liberated figures for whom the author's sympathies and admiration are profound.

The ultimate problem in Virginia Woolf's historical perspective is that of violence and war, especially as they imply the question of man's progress or decline in the history of European civilization. *Between the Acts* addresses itself, implicitly and explicitly, to the question of how far, if at all, man has evolved from the apes and it is significant that just as Mrs. Swithin is introduced to us by way of her interest in England's prehistoric past, when England and the Continent were one, the last time we meet her is on the penultimate page of the novel as she reads in her *Outline of History* that ''Prehistoric man . . . half-human, half-ape, roused himself from his semi-crouching position and raised great stones'' (*B*, p. 218). What is clear is Virginia Woolf's especial intention in this final novel of manners to juxtapose the veneer of social mode and polish with ambivalent and, at best, barely repressed hostilities which, in turn, conjure up the unleashed violence of World War across the Channel. One sees an earlier concern with war in *The Years* and in the dead hero of *Jacob's Room* and the shell-shocked Septimus Smith of *Mrs. Dalloway,* but only in this concluding opus does Woolf seem to have felt compelled to evoke and explore the psychological climate and long history of war and violence.

At several points in the novel human beings are described in terms of their direct resemblance to animals. Mrs. Haines is depicted as ''a goosefaced woman'' who sees ''something to gobble in the gutter'' (*B*, p. 3) while Isa Oliver and Rupert Haines are compared to two swans, one ''with a tangle of dirty duckweed'' and the other with ''webbed feet'' (*B*, p. 5) entangled by her husband. Bart Oliver is seen by little George to be ''a terrible peaked eyeless monster moving on legs'' (*B*, pp. 11–12) who ''growled'' (*B*, p. 21) at his sister, and in the final scene we see his skin shudder like his dog's as ''He rose, shook himself . . . and stalked from the room'' (*B*, p. 218). The effects of war on the Continent are paralleled by the guards' bestial rape of a girl in the barrack room at Whitehall (which the author details with extraordinary vividness and about which the Oliver family reads in *The Times*), and this uncontrolled, animal sexuality has a kind of counterpart in the intense, barely controlled attractions of both William Dodge and Mrs. Manresa to the hirsute, blond, and blue-eyed Giles, who, following the ''wild child of nature,'' arouses in his wife in turn both hate and love.

Giles Oliver's irrational and impassioned hostility to Dodge, whose sexual proclivities he intuits, reveals itself in what is undoubtedly the single most shocking and graphic scene in the book as he kicks a stone which is specified as "barbaric" and "prehistoric": "He played it alone. The gate was a goal; to be reached in ten. The first kick was Manresa (lust). The second, Dodge (perversion). The third, himself (coward)" (*B*, pp. 98–99). With the tenth step he reaches a snake which is choking on a toad in its mouth; the snake cannot swallow nor the toad die. His impulsive response is to stamp on them: "The mass crushed and slithered. The white canvas on his tennis shoes was bloodstained and sticky. But it was action. Action relieved him" (*B*, p. 99). The author has at once brilliantly depicted the need to release hostility, including that masochistic strain directed to oneself and involving personal sexual inhibitions and fears, and reminded us that such impulses and needs are to be found not only among German warriors but also English gentlemen wearing blazers, flannels, and white tennis shoes.

In an immensely powerful and persuasive essay which she wrote in August, 1940, while *Between the Acts* was in progress, and entitled "Thoughts on Peace in an Air Raid," Virginia Woolf concerns herself, in essay form, with the same problems of violence, war, hostility, and the subconscious. It was written during the many air raids which the Woolfs suffered in their country home in Sussex after their two homes in London had been almost entirely destroyed, and, like *Between the Acts,* the scope of the Essay goes back in memory to the past, "the memory of other Augusts—in Bayreuth, listening to Wagner; in Rome, walking over the Campagna; in London" (*DM*, pp. 211–212). Stressing the fact that the "enemy" is not simply or exclusively the German, she turns her attention to all the Giles Olivers in Britain: "We must help the young Englishmen to root out from themselves the love of medals and decorations. We must create more honourable activities for those who try to conquer in themselves their fighting instinct, their subconscious Hitlerism. We must compensate the man for the loss of his gun" (*DM*, p. 211).

At the end of *Between the Acts* night has come again, both the immediate end of daylight and, possibly, the night of an historic epoch. The last thought which Isa murmurs to herself is the ominous: "This year, last year, next year, never . . ." (*B*, p. 217). Giles and Isa are alone and silent: "Alone, enmity was bared; also love. Before they slept, they must fight; after they had fought, they would embrace. From that embrace another life might be born. But first they must fight, as the dog fox fights with the vixen, in the heart of darkness, in the fields of night" (*B*, p. 219). The continuity of life and culture is affirmed, however cautiously, and the inevitability of historical cycle, which includes fighting as well as loving and the possibility of the conception of new life, is accepted. Significantly, Woolf emphasizes that *first* they *must* fight, and her stress recalls Thomas Mann's in *The Magic Mountain* where, in the final moment of the novel, he implies that only in the fires of destruction can one possibly hope for the renewal of life and the rebirth of love. The specific details about the house Pointz Hall and the immediate situation are transcended, and the scene suddenly takes on the kind of archetypal dimensions which we have seen in the earlier novels:

> The great hooded chairs had become enormous. And Giles too. And Isa too against the window. The window was all sky without colour. The house had lost its shelter. It was night before roads were made, or houses. It was the night that dwellers in caves had watched from some high place among rocks.
>
> Then the curtain rose. They spoke (*B*, p. 219).

Significantly, the last sentence of the book is "They spoke," and the act of speech both marks a necessary beginning and reminds us of man's starting point in civilization and the ultimate capacity which distinguishes him from the animal world. The same kind of resolution through man's capacity for speech is seen as well in "Thoughts on Peace in an Air Raid," where Virginia Woolf describes the safe landing during World War II of a German pilot in a Sussex field: "He said to his captors, speaking fairly good English, 'How glad I am that the fight is over!' Then an Englishman gave him a cigarette, and an Englishwoman made him a cup of tea. That would seem to show that if you can free the man from the machine, the seed does not fall upon altogether stony ground. The seed may be fertile" (*DM,* p. 212).

Leonard Woolf mentioned to me how he could not understand why *Between the Acts* starts all over again at the end.[7] Is it not because the author's vision saw that each ending in turn implies, like the end of *The Waves* and *The Years,* a new beginning—of the day tomorrow and, possibly, of a new historical "moment"? We know from the *Diary* and Leonard Woolf's *Autobiography* that it was psychologically imperative for Woolf always to have several works in progress, including a novel, which would provide the necessary and personal sense of continuity in her own life and work, and *Anon* was the working title of the project which was to succeed *Between the Acts*.

In this context one of the most moving scenes is that which foreshadows the final one as we see the outcast artist, Miss La Trobe, as she sits alone in the pub after the pageant, exhausted, but already planning her next production, which will include two figures, on whom "The curtain would rise" (*B*, p. 210). Her own crisis as an artist and individual is transcended through the continuity of new life which the word provides: "Words of one syllable sank down into the mud. She

---

[7]In an interview at the Hogarth Press, London, on September 25, 1962.

drowsed; she nodded. The mud became fertile. Words rose above the intolerably laden dumb oxen plodding through the mud. Words without meaning—wonderful words" (*B*, p. 212).

Earlier in this essay we saw how Virginia Woolf wondered in 1929 if "it may be that though we change, one flying after another, so quick, so quick, yet we are somehow successive and continuous we human beings," and the *Diary* records how three years later, in 1932, she and Leonard had discussed death, "the second time this year: how we may be like worms crushed by a motor car: what does the worm know of the car—how it is made? There may be a reason: if so not one we, as human beings, can grasp" (*D*, August 5, p. 179). Both statements reveal an agony about the human condition and its limitations and also a profound humility and orientation to faith. Both show the juxtaposition in Virginia Woolf's mind of her shock over the finality and waste of death with a kind of suspension of disbelief and judgment and a hesitation to pronounce a final word with any certainty. The figures of the worm and motor car convey (like Virginia Woolf's insanity-caused suicide) the existentialist vision of the absurd which inspired Tertullian's humble statement of belief, "Credo quia absurdum est." Both Virginia Woolf's and Tertullian's leaps of faith, precarious as they are, imply a nonanthropocentric view of the universe. In short we see the same kind of projection of thought and perspective into an indefinite future which pervades this author's entire career and especially *Between the Acts,* and implicit in this novel is the suggestion that a victorious German invasion, if it takes place, will, like the many conquests of Britain over the centuries, be absorbed as part of her evolution.

In the undated essay, "Evening over Sussex: Reflections in a Motor Car," the different "selves" of the author pull her thought in various directions. One of these "selves" dangles from the future and thinks of "Sussex in five hundred years to come." After specifying such technical achievements of the future as "magic gates," "draughts fan-blown by electric power," and "lights intense and firmly directed" which will go over the earth and do the work, her prophesy envisions how "By day and by night Sussex in five centuries will be full of charming thoughts, quick, effective beams" (*DM*, p. 15). On the one hand, the prophesy seems both fanciful and yet founded on inevitable scientific achievement. On the other, it shows the extent to which Virginia Woolf's deeply rooted historical consciousness became the springboard for belief and her orientation to the future. The timeless moments which comprised, for both Eliot and Virginia Woolf, a pattern of history offered redemption from time and affirmed finally a continuum into the future.

Selected Bibliography

I PRINCIPAL WORKS OF VIRGINIA WOOLF

While the following bibliography is extensive, it is by no means exhaustive: it covers only Woolf's major works. The most comprehensive record of her writing may be found in B. J. Kirkpatrick's *A Bibliography of Virginia Woolf* (London: Rupert Hart-Davis, 1957; revised 1967). Kirkpatrick's bibliography offers readers an interesting history of the printing of each book and essay that Woolf published. The Hogarth Press in London publishes a uniform edition of Virginia Woolf's volumes. Her publisher in the United States is Harcourt Brace Jovanovich. Those volumes marked with an asterisk are currently available in paperback in the United States.

The Voyage Out. (London: Duckworth, 1915; New York: Doran, 1920; New York: Harcourt, Brace, 1926.)

Night and Day. (London: Duckworth, 1919; New York: Doran, 1920.)

Jacob's Room. (Richmond, England: Hogarth Press, 1922; New York: Harcourt, Brace, 1923.)

The Common Reader. (London: Hogarth Press, 1925; New York: Harcourt, Brace, 1925.)

Mrs. Dalloway. (London: Hogarth Press, 1925; New York: Harcourt, Brace, 1925.)

To the Lighthouse. (London: Hogarth Press, 1927; New York: Harcourt, Brace, 1927.)

Orlando: A Biography. (London: Hogarth Press, 1928; New York: Crosby Gaige, 1928; New York: Harcourt, Brace, 1929.)

A Room of One's Own. (London: Hogarth Press, 1929; New York: Fountain Press, 1929; New York: Harcourt, Brace, 1929.)

The Waves. (London: Hogarth Press, 1931; New York: Harcourt, Brace, 1931.)

The Common Reader: Second Series. (London: Hogarth Press, 1932; New York: Harcourt, Brace, 1932.)

*Flush: A Biography. (London: Hogarth Press, 1933; New York: Harcourt, Brace, 1933.)

*The Years. (London: Hogarth Press, 1937; New York: Harcourt, Brace, 1937.)

*Three Guineas. (London: Hogarth Press, 1938; New York: Harcourt, Brace, 1938.)

Roger Fry: A Biography. (London: Hogarth Press, 1940; New York: Harcourt, Brace, 1940.)

*Between the Acts. (London: Hogarth Press, 1941; New York: Harcourt, Brace, 1941.)

The Death of the Moth and Other Essays. (London: Hogarth Press, 1942; New York: Harcourt, Brace, 1942.)

*A Haunted House and Other Stories. (London: Hogarth Press, 1944; New York: Harcourt, Brace, 1944.)

The Moment and Other Essays. (London: Hogarth Press, 1947; New York: Harcourt, Brace, 1947.)

*The Captain's Death Bed and Other Essays. (London: Hogarth Press, 1950; New York: Harcourt, Brace, 1950.)

*A Writer's Diary. (London: Hogarth Press, 1953; New York: Harcourt, Brace, 1954.)

Virginia Woolf and Lytton Strachey: Letters. Edited by Leonard Woolf and James Strachey. (London: Hogarth Press and Chatto & Windus, 1956; New York: Harcourt, Brace, 1956.)

Granite and Rainbow: Essays. (London: Hogarth Press, 1958; New York: Harcourt, Brace, 1958.)

Contemporary Writers. Edited by Jean Guiget. (London: Hogarth Press, 1965.)

Collected Essays (4 vols.) (London: Hogarth Press, 1967; New York: Harcourt, Brace, 1967.)

Mrs. Dalloway's Party: A Short Story Sequence. Edited by Stella McNichol. (London: Hogarth Press, 1973.)

II SECONDARY SOURCES–GENERAL

With a few exceptions, I have limited this section of the bibliography to books about Virginia Woolf's fiction in general. Books that deal with specific texts are included in the next section.

Bazin, Nancy Topping. *Virginia Woolf and the Androgynous Vision*. (New Brunswick, N. J.: Rutgers University Press, 1973.)

Beja, Morris. *Epiphany in the Modern Novel*. (Seattle: University of Washington Press, 1971.)

Bennett, Joan. *Virginia Woolf: Her Art as a Novelist*. (New York: Harcourt, Brace, 1945.)

Blackstone, Bernard. *Virginia Woolf: A Commentary*. (New York: Harcourt, Brace, 1949.)

Brewster, Dorothy. *Virginia Woolf*. (New York: Gotham Library, 1962.)
———. *Virginia Woolf's London*. (London: Allen & Unwin, 1969.)

Chambers, R. L. *The Novels of Virginia Woolf*. (Edinburgh and London: Oliver and Boyd, 1947.)

Daiches, David. *Virginia Woolf*. (Norfolk, Conn.: New Directions, 1942.)

Edel, Leon. *The Psychological Novel, 1900–1950*. (New York: Lippincott, 1955.)Forster, E. M. *Virginia Woolf*. (New York: Harcourt,

Forster, E. M. *Virginia Woolf*. (New York: Harcourt, Brace, 1942.) [Reprinted in Forster's *Two Cheers for Democracy* (New York: Harcourt, Brace, 1952), pp. 242–258.]

Graham, John. "Time in the Novels of Virginia Woolf," *University of Toronto Quarterly*, xviii (January, 1949), 186–201.

Gruber, Ruth. *Virginia Woolf: A Study*. (Leipzig: Tauchnitz, 1935.)

Guiget, Jean. *Virginia Woolf and Her Works*. Translated by Jean Stuart. (New York: Harcourt, Brace, 1966.)

Hafley, James. *The Glass Roof: Virginia Woolf As Novelist*. (Berkeley: University of California Press, 1954.)

Holtby, Winifred. *Virginia Woolf*. (London: Wishart, 1932.)

Johnstone, J. K. *The Bloomsbury Group: A Study of E. M. Forster, Lytton Strachey, Virginia Woolf, and Their Circle*. (London: Secker & Warburg, 1954.)

Kirkpatrick, B. J. *A Bibliography of Virginia Woolf*. (London: Rupert Hart-Davis, 1957; revised 1967.)

Latham, Jacqueline E. M. (ed.). *Critics on Virginia Woolf*. (London: Allen & Unwin, 1970.)

Love, Jean O. *Worlds of Consciousness: Mythopoetic Thought in the Novels of Virginia Woolf*. (Berkeley: University of California Press, 1970.)

McLaurin, Allen. *Virginia Woolf: The Echoes Enslaved*. (Cambridge, England: Cambridge University Press, 1973.)

Marder, Herbert. *Feminism and Art: A Study of Virginia Woolf*. (Chicago and London: University of Chicago Press, 1968.)

Moody, A. D. *Virginia Woolf*. (New York: Grove Press, 1963.)

Nathan, Monique. *Virginia Woolf*. Translated by Herma Briffault. (New York: Evergreen Books, 1961.)

Naremore, James. *The World Without a Self, Virginia Woolf and the Novel.* (New Haven and London: Yale University Press, 1973.)

Newton, Deborah. *Virginia Woolf.* (Melbourne: Melbourne University Press, 1946.)

Noble, Joan Russell (ed.). *Recollections of Virginia Woolf by Her Contemporaries.* (New York: William Morrow, 1972.)

Osawa, Nimoru. *Virginia Woolf.* (Tokyo: Nanundo, 1956.)

Richter, Harvena. *Virginia Woolf: The Inward Voyage.* (Princeton, Princeton University Press, 1970.)

Sprague, Claire (ed.). *Virginia Woolf: A Collection of Critical Essays.* (Englewood Cliffs, N. J.: Prentice-Hall, 1971.)

Thakur, N. C. *The Symbolism of Virginia Woolf.* (London and New York: Oxford University Press, 1965.)

Trautmann, Joanne. *The Jessamy Brides: The Friendship of Virginia Woolf and V. Sackville West.* (University Park, Pa.: Pennsylvania State University Press, 1973.)

Woodring, Carl. *Virginia Woolf.* (New York: Columbia University Press, 1966.)

III SECONDARY SOURCES ABOUT SPECIFIC WORKS

Between the Acts

Fox, Stephen D. "The Fish Pond as Symbolic Center in *Between the Acts.*" *Modern Fiction Studies,* 18 (Autumn, 1972), 467–473.

Watkins, Renée. "Survival in Discontinuity: Virginia Woolf's *Between the Acts.*" *Massachusetts Review,* 10 (Spring, 1969), 356–376.

Wilkinson, Ann Y. "A Principle of Unity in *Between the Acts.*" *Criticism,* 8 (Winter, 1966), 53–63.

Zorn, Marilyn. "The Pageant in *Between the Acts.*" *Modern Fiction Studies,* 2 (February, 1956), 31–35.

Flush

Szladits, Lola L. " 'The Life, Character and Opinion of Flush the Spaniel.' " *Bulletin of The New York Public Library,* 74 (1970), 211–218.

A Haunted House and Other Stories

Baldesschwiler, Eileen. "The Lyric Short Story: Sketch of a History." *Studies in Short Fiction,* 6 (Summer, 1969) 443–453.

Chapman, R. T. *"The Lady in the Looking-Glass:* Modes of Perception in a Short Story by Virginia Woolf.*" Modern Fiction Studies,* 18 (Autumn, 1972), 331—337.

Hafley, James. "On One of Virginia Woolf's Short Stories." *Modern Fiction Studies,* 2 (February, 1956), 13–16.

Jacob's Room

Morgenstern, Barry. "The Self-Conscious Narrator in *Jacob's Room." Modern Fiction Studies,* 18 (Autumn, 1972), 351–361.

Mrs. Dalloway

Benjamin, Anna. "Towards an Understanding of the Meaning of Virginia Woolf's *Mrs. Dalloway." Wisconsin Studies in Contemporary Literature,* 6 (Summer, 1965), 214–223.

Gamble, Isabel. "The Secret Sharer in *Mrs. Dalloway." Accent,* 16 (Autumn, 1956), 235–251.

Gelfant, Blanche. "Love and Conversion in *Mrs. Dalloway." Criticism,* 8 (Summer, 1966), 229–245.

Hoffmann, Charles G. "The Real Mrs. Dalloway." *University of Kansas City Review, 22 (Spring, 1956), 204*–208.

———. "From Short Story to Novel: The Manuscript Revisions of Virginia Woolf's *Mrs. Dalloway." Modern Fiction Studies,* 14 (Summer, 1968), 171–186.

Lewis, A. J. "From 'The Hours' to *Mrs. Dalloway." British Museum Quarterly,* 28 (Summer, 1964), 15–18.

Miller, J. Hillis. "Virginia Woolf's All Soul's Day: The Omniscient Narrator in *Mrs. Dalloway."* In *The Shaken Realist: Essays in Modern Literature in Honor of Frederick J. Hoffman,* Melvin J. Friedman and John B. Vickery (eds.) (Baton Rouge: Louisiana State University Press, 1970.)

Night and Day

Cummings, Melinda Feldt. *"Night and Day:* Virginia Woolf's Visionary Synthesis of Reality." *Modern Fiction Studies,* 18 (Autumn, 1972), 339–349.

Orlando

Baldanza, Frank. *"Orlando* and the Sackvilles." *PMLA,* 70 (March, 1955), 274–279.

German, Howard and Sharon Kaehele. "The Dialectic of Time in *Orlando.*" *College English,* 24 (1962), 35–41.

Graham, J. W. " 'The Caricature Value' of Parody and Fantasy in *Orlando.*" *University of Toronto Quarterly,* 30 (July, 1961), 345–366.

Hoffmann, Charles G. "Fact and Fantasy in *Orlando:* Virginia Woolf's Manuscript Revisions." *Texas Studies in Literature and Language,* 10 (Fall, 1968), 435–444.

Samuelson, Ralph. "Virginia Woolf: *Orlando* and the Feminist Spirit." *Western Humanities Review,* 15 (Winter, 1961), 51–58.

To the Lighthouse

Auerbach, Erich. "The Brown Stocking." In *Mimesis: The Representation of Reality in Western Literature,* translated by Willard R. Trask. (Princeton: Princeton University Press, 1953), pp. 525–541 and 551–552.

Beja, Morris. *Virginia Woolf:* To the Lighthouse: *A Casebook.* (London: Macmillan, 1970.)

Leaska, Mitchell A. *Virginia Woolf's Lighthouse: A Study in Critical Method.* (New York: Columbia University Press, 1970.)

May, Keith M. "The Symbol of Painting in Virginia Woolf's *To the Lighthouse.*" *Review of English Literature,* 8 (April 1967), 91–98.

Proudfit, Sharon Wood. "Lily Briscoe's Painting: A Key to Personal Relations in *To the Lighthouse.*" *Criticism,* 13 (Winter, 1971), 26–39.

Vogler, Thomas A., ed. *Twentieth Century Interpretations of* To the Lighthouse. (Englewood Cliffs, N. J.: Prentice-Hall, 1970.)

The Voyage Out

Leaska, Mitchell A. "Virginia Woolf's *The Voyage Out:* Character Deduction and the Function of Ambiguity." *Virginia Woolf Quarterly,* 1 (Winter, 1973), 18–41.

The Waves

Collins, Robert G. *Virginia Woolf's Black Arrows of Sensation: "The Waves."* (Ilfracombe, England: A. H. Stockwell, 1962.)

Gorsky, Susan. " 'The Central Shadow': Characterization in *The Waves.*" *Modern Fiction Studies,* 18 (Autumn, 1972), 449–466.

Payne, Michael. "The Eclipse of Order: The Ironic Structure of *The Waves.*" *Modern Fiction Studies,* 15 (Summer, 1969), 209–218.

Raantavaara, Irma. "Virginia Woolf's *The Waves*." Helsingfors: *Societas Scietiarum Fennica, Commentationes Huminarum Litterarum,* 26, 2 (1960).

The Years

Hoffmann, Charles G. "Virginia Woolf's Manuscript Revisions of *The Years*." *PMLA,* 84 (January, 1969), 79–89.
Marder, Herbert. "Beyond the Lighthouse: *The Years*." *Bucknell Review,* 15 (March, 1967), 61–70.

IV: BIOGRAPHIES AND MEMOIRS

Bell, Quentin. *Virginia Woolf: A Biography*. (New York: Harcourt, Brace, 1972.)
Noble, Joan Russell (ed.). *Recollections of Virginia Woolf by Her Contemporaries*. (New York: William Morrow, 1972.)
Woolf, Leonard. *Sowing: An Autobiography of the Years 1880–1904*. (New York: Harcourt, Brace, 1960.)
———. *Growing: An Autobiography of the Years 1904–1911*. (New York: Harcourt, Brace, 1962.)
———. *Beginning Again: An Autobiography of the Years 1911–1918*. (New York: Harcourt, Brace, 1964.)
———. *Downhill All the Way: An Autobiography of the Years 1919–1939*. (New York: Harcourt, Brace, 1967.)
———. *The Journey Not the Arrival Matters: An Autobiography of the Years 1939–1969*. (New York: Harcourt, Brace, 1970.)

Catalog

If you are interested in a list of fine Paperback
books, covering a wide range of subjects
and interests, send your name and address,
requesting your free catalog, to:

McGraw-Hill Paperbacks
1221 Avenue of Americas
New York, N. Y. 10020